MY DAILY HORUS SCOPE

MY DAILY HORUS SCOPE

Calendar translation by Diana Janeen Pierce
Art work and design by Ramona Louise Wheeler

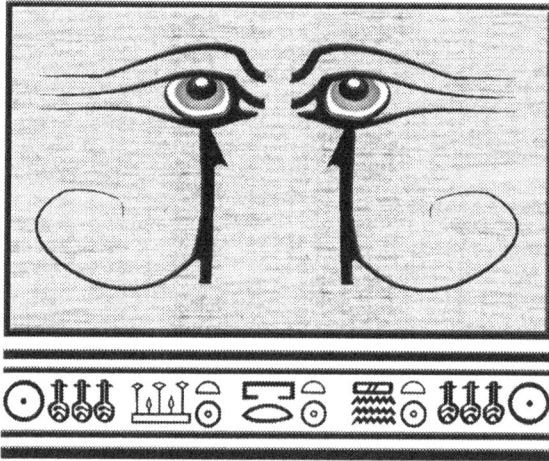

WILDSIDE PRESS

My Daily Horus Scope

A publication of Wildside Press
www.wildsidepress.com

FIRST EDITION

PERSONAL DATA:

AN EGYPTIAN STYLE JOURNAL

The dates on these pages are arranged according to the ancient Egyptian calendar. Each page begins with the modern date because we are accustomed to our own calendar. One can easily become lost trying to work through the year purely in Egyptian. These dates are, however, only markers in time. The journey is yours. The modern date is followed by the day count of the Egyptian month and the "omen" of the day. There are three such omens for each day, morning, afternoon and night. Days are most often either ☉𓀀𓀀𓀀 or ☉𓂝𓂝𓂝. Variations such as ☉𓂝𓂝𓀀 indicate, for example, a day that starts out with difficulty but ends well. These signs have been interpreted differently in other translations, as "lucky and unlucky," "good and bad," "fortunate and unfortunate." Such translation does, however, give a false impression of the original intention. The sign 𓄤 means "beautiful," "pleasing," or "wonderful." The 𓂝 is an arm upraised and holding a shield, and has been translated as "opposing," "battle," "struggle," "difficult." It is, therefore, not quite appropriate to simplify the use of these terms in the calendar as simply "lucky or unlucky." The Egyptians themselves apparently had a different use for their horoscope. You should apply "beautiful" or "pleasing" and "difficult" or "a struggle," according to your own personal assessments of your day.

Each day had its own divine guardian, its *"natur."* These gods, or *natur,* (plural *naturu*; feminine *naturit, naturitu*) are there to be the representatives of the divine on Earth and of the human in heaven. You direct the prayers and conversation of the day to the divinity of the day, and you recieve from this divinity the theme for your meditations of the day.

The Egyptian system is set up as three seasons with four months, and each month has thirty days. Each of those thirty days has its own name. The deity and the name of the day are the same for every month. The leftover five days were given to the most sacred festivals of the entire year. The Yearly Five Days, as they were known, were outside of the calendar and outside of time, five days of eternity that link the end of the old year and the beginning of the new. In these five days the divine beings who are the parents of humanity are born.

You will notice that there is no modern year given for this journal. Unlike the modern calendar, the date of the month and the name of the day remain linked. The first of every month will always be the day named "New Month Day." The sixth day will always be "Sixth Day." Day twelve will always be "Making Love." You will find, therefore, that this journal becomes a still point in time, the unchanging map by which you navigate through the years. That was the primary intention of the ancients. What began as a means of tracking the rise and fall of the Nile River became the navigation system of the ebb and flow of the human psyche through time. Unless you have a great deal to say each day, this journal should keep track of your life for several years. Write the year at the beginning of each entry and you will be able to compare the patterns and progress of your life from year to year, one day at a time. For this reason, you can begin this journal on any day of the year. Write the year and indicate that page as the beginning. There is an extra page at the end that can be used for the Leap Year—the one piece of calendar technology which the Egyptians missed.

Below is a grid explaining the arrangement of the Egyptian calendar and horoscope material on each page. At the very top of each page you will find the ancient Egyptian calendar date, using the name of the Egyptian month, the modern dates which it covers, and the name of the season to which that month belongs. The figure at the bottom corner of the page is the divinity of that month.

The original papyri which D. J. Pierce translated did have some damaged and missing sections. These are indicated by (Lost...) or (omission.) Even these, however, can be an interesting comment on the day.

ANCIENT MONTH AND SEASON,   THE MODERN DATES OF THAT MONTH

Modern Date   DAY OF THE MONTH   Symbol of day's quality.
Name of the day in Egyptian   Divine guardian of this day.
Instructions for this day.
  "Auspice for this day."
    Sacred days and religious festivals here in italic.

More detailed explanations of the calendar round and of the ancient Egyptian divinities and their religion are available in the companion volume:

Walk Like An Egyptian: A Modern Guide To The Religion And Philosophy Of Ancient Egypt, Third Edition, Expanded, Including The Ancient Egyptian Calendar, by Ramona Louise Wheeler, published by Wildside Press, www.wildsidepress.com. It is available in paperback and hardback editions.

Modern Dates For The Nile Rising Calendar

Akhet, season of The Inundation, June 27 to October 24.
   The deity is Hapy, the Nile in flood.

· *Thuthy*	June 27 to July 26.
· *Paopy*	July 27 to August 25.
· *Hathys*	August 26 to September 24.
· *Choiach*	September 25 to October 24

Poret, season of The Emergence, October 25 to February 21.
   The deity is Khopry, the Rising Sun.

· *Tyby*	October 25 to November 23.
· *Menchir*	November 24 to December 23.
· *Famenoth*	December 24 to January 22.
· *Parmuthy*	January 23 to February 21

Shomu, season of The Harvest, February 22 to June 21.
   The deity is Re, the creator of consciousness and space/time.

· *Pachons*	February 22 to March 23.
· *Paony*	March 24 to April 22.
· *Epipy*	April 23 to May 22.
· *Mesore*	May 23 to June 21.

The Names And The Divine Guardians Of The Months

Akhet, season of Hapy.

Thuthy.	The deity is Thoth.
Paopy.	The deity is Ptah.
Hathys.	The deity is Hathor.
Choiach.	The deity is Sakhmet.

Poret, season of Khopry.

Tyby.	The deity is Min.
Menchir.	The deity is *Rekeh-Ur.*
Famenoth.	The deity is *Rekeh-Netches.*
Parmuthy.	The deity is *Rennetet.*

Shomu, season of Re.

Pachons.	The deity is Khonsu.
Paony.	The deity is *Khenthy.*
Epipy.	The deity is *Ipt.*
Mesore.	The deity is Horus Of The Two Horizons.

1. **New Month Day.** Thoth is the deity.
2. **New Crescent Day.** Horus is the deity.
3. **Arrival Day.** Osiris is the deity.
4. **Zem Priests Emerge.** Isis is the deity.
5. **Altar Offerings Day.** Hapy is the deity.
6. **Sixth Day.** Star Of His Mother is the deity.
7. **First Quarter Day.** Qebsennuf is the deity.
8. **Main Emergence.** Ma'atet-f is the deity.
9. **Hidden One.** He Does The Talking is the deity.
10. **He Who Protects His Royal Name.**
    He Makes His Name Himself is the deity.
11. **Great Lady Protector.** Sakhmet is the deity.
12. **Love Making.** Bring The Advocate is the deity.
13. **Approach of Re.** Re is the deity.
14. **Progress Of The Ba.** Consider The *Ba* is the deity.
15. **Half Month Day.** Amauai is the deity.
16. **Two Houses Fight.** Horus, Sutekh are the deities.
17. **Second Arrival Day.** Re is the deity.
18. **Moon Day.** Ahi The Moon is the deity.
19. **Hear His Commands.**
    Bring His Mother is the deity.
20. **Offering Meat.** Opener Of The Ways is the deity.
21. **Apru's Day.** Anubis is the deity.
22. **Passing Of Sopdut.** *Nai* is the deity.
23. **Last Quarter Day.** *Na-Ur* is the deity.
24. **Darkness.** Nekhbet is the deity.
25. **Departing.** Shem is the deity.
26. **House Of Appearances.** *Ma'atef-f* is the deity.
27. **Funeral Offerings.** Khnum is the deity.
28. **Jubilee Of The Sky.** Nut is the deity.
29. **Weakness.** *Utettef-f* is the deity.
30. **Awaken.** Horus Advocates For Him is the deity.

The Yearly Five Days Between The End Of The Past Year And The Beginning Of The New Year
June 22 to June 26

An Introduction To The Beginning Of Infinity And The End Of Eternity Which The *Naturu* And *Naturitu* Of The Shrine And The Assembly Of The *Paut Naturu* Have Made, And Which The Majesty Of Thoth Has Gathered Together In The Great House (*Per-Ur*) In The Presence Of The Lord Of The Universe (Re). What Has Been Found In The Library In The Rear House (*Per-Ha*) Of The *Paut Naturu*. House Of Re (*Per-Re*), House Of Osiris (*Per-Osiris*), House Of Horus (*Per-Horu*.)

Charm To Be Spoken:

Say these words at sunrise on the first day:

"The Great Ones are born. As for the Great Ones whose forms are not mysterious, beware of them. Their occasion or deeds will not come.

Birth of Osiris!
Birth of the Original Horus!
Birth of Sutekh!
Birth of Isis!
Birth of Lady Of The House!

I, who know the names of the days, will not hunger. I will not thirst, and Bastet will not overpower me. I will not enter into the Great Law Court. I will not die through an enemy of the pharaoh, and will not die through the pestilence of the year. I will last every day until death arrives. No illness will take possession of me. I, who know them, (i.e., the names of the days,) will prosper, and my speech is important to listen to in the presence of Re."

(Repeat the above charm each day, adding the appropriate name of the *natur* or *naturit* born on that day.)

June 22

The Pure One   Lord Osiris is born.

The Birth of Osiris.

Words to be said on this day:

"Oh, Osiris, bull in his cavern whose name is hidden, child of his mother, hail to you! Hail to you! I am your son, oh, father Osiris.

The name of this day is: *The Pure One.*"

June 23

Powerful Is The Heart   Horus The Original is born.

The Birth of the Original Horus.

Words to be said on this day:

"Oh, Horus Of The Spirit! It is repeated anew. It will provide good protection because of it, you make (lost...)

The name of this day is: *Powerful Is The Heart.*"

June 24

Powerful Of Arm

Sutekh is born.

The Birth of Sutekh.

Words to be said on this day:

"Oh, Sutekh, son of Nut, great of strength, protection is in your hands of holiness. I am the son of your son.

The name of this day is: *Powerful Of Arm.*"

June 25
He Who Makes Terror   Lady Isis is born.

The Birth of Isis.

Words to be said on this day:

"Oh, Isis, daughter of Nut the Eldest, Mistress Of Magic, provider of the book, mistress who appeases the Dual Dimensions, her face is glorious. I am the brother and the sister."

The name of this day is: *He Who Makes Terror.*"

June 26   ☉⚕⚕⚕

The Child Who Is In His Nest   Lady Of The House is born.

The Birth of Lady Of The House.

Words to be said on this day:

"Oh, Lady Of The House, daughter of Nut, sister of Sutekh, she whose father sees a healthy daughter, stable of face, stable of face. I am divine power in the womb of my mother Nut.

The name of this day is: *The Child Who Is In His Nest.*"

These words are to be spoken over a protective amulet on the last day before sunset. Draw the images of Osiris, The Original Horus, Sutekh, Isis and Lady Of The House on fine linen and place it around your neck. Then say four times:

"Hail to you, oh, Great Ones according to your names, children of the *naturitu* who came forth from the sacred womb, *naturu* because their father, *naturitu* because of their mother, without yet knowing eternity.

Behold! May you make protection! May you happen again, and may you protect me, for I am one who is on their list.

This charm is called: Self-dedication Contract."

ADDITIONAL NOTES ON THE YEARLY FIVE DAYS:

THUTHY

Thoth is the *natur* of this month.

FIRST MONTH OF THE SEASON OF AKHET
AND THE BEGINNING OF THE NEW YEAR

June 27   DAY ONE

New Month Day   Thoth

This is the first day of the New Year.

"At the beginning of the high Nile there is washing throughout the whole land. They say it comes in form of fresh Nun. The *naturu* and *naturitu* are in great festivity on this day, and all others."

The birth of Re. First Day of Thuthy.

(*Note:* This is one of the rare references to the rituals for Re on New Year's Day. Everyone in Egypt bathed in the Nile this day. Nun is the Cosmic waters.)

June 28   DAY TWO   ☉ 𓏏𓏏𓏏

New Crescent Day   Horus

  Anything you see will be good.

"It is the day the *Paut Naturu* goes before Re. Their hearts are pleased at seeing his youthfulness after they destroyed Apophis, who rebelled against their master, and for overcoming Re's foe, wherever he might be, so that he might fall on his back amidst the flood."

June 29   DAY THREE   ⊙⚱⚱☊☌

Arrival Day   Osiris

A crocodile will kill those born today.
"It is the day of making *ipy* (possibly dykes) in the river by the *naturu*."
The Birth of Aton.

June 30   DAY FOUR

Zem Priests Emerge   Isis

Do not navigate in or travel by boat. Do nothing today.

"It is the day Hathor emerges, accompanied by her executioners, the *khatbu*, to the riverbank. The *naturu* sail in an opposing wind."

(Note: This refers to the attempt at the destruction of humanind.)

July 1   DAY FIVE   ☉☥☥☥

Altar Offerings Day   Hapy

   Anything you see will be good.
"The *naturu* are peaceful in heaven sailing in the Day Boat Of Re."

July 2 · DAY SIX · 𒀭𒀭𒀭𒀭𒀭

Sixth Day · Star Of His Mother

Anyone born on this day will die by the trampling of a bull.
(Lost...)

Monthly feast of Re.

THOTH

July 3   DAY SEVEN   ☉⌂⌂⌂⌂

First Quarter Day   Qebsenuf

Anything you see will be good.

"It is the day of welcoming the Nile and making offerings to the *naturu*."

July 4   DAY EIGHT
Main Emergence   Ma'atef-f

Spend this day on the water. Do not go out this night.
"Because Re emerges (lost...) As for him who navigates Nun, and as for anyone
who is shipwrecked at sea (lost...)"

July 5   DAY NINE

Hidden One   He Does The Talking.

Anything you see will be good.

"This day the hearts of those who are in the horizon are pacifed in the presence of the majesty of Re."

July 6   DAY TEN ☉ 🜨

He Who Protects His Royal Name   He Makes A Name Himself.

Those born today will die of honorable old age.

"It is the day of the going forth to the House Of Peace, while the *naturu* and *naturitu* are in festivity."

The Second Monthly Feast Of Re.

July 7   DAY ELEVEN   ⊙ ꜣꜣꜣꜣꜣꜣ
Great Lady Protector   Sakhmet

   Kindle fire on this day. Do not look at a bull, and do not make love on this day.

"Today the Great Flame (The *Wadjet* Eye) is in a rage in the Inaccessible Shrine. (Lost...) who are in the following of his Majesty Re."

   (*Note*: the Inaccessible Shrine is the Shrine Of The Boat found in the back of the House Of Life.)

July 8   DAY TWELVE   ⊙ 𓄿𓂝𓄿𓂝𓄿𓂝

Making Love   Bring The Advocate.

   Do not go out until Re sets in his horizon.

"It is the day Re exchanges his oarsmen one for another. Anyone who disobeys Re falls down at once."

(Note: At sunset and dawn Re's crew, the oarsmen of the Evening and the Morning Boats, exchanged duty at the oars.)

July 9   DAY THIRTEEN

Approach of Re   Re

   Anyone born on this day will die blind.

"It is the day of the slaughter by Neith."

July 10   DAY FOURTEEN   (Lost...)
Progress Of The Ba   Consider The Ba.
   The birth of Re.
"Make offering to your local *naturu*."

July 11   DAY FIFTEEN
Half Month Day   Amauai

Avoid boats today. Do not continue traveling in a boat.
"It is a day of Sutekh's rage. One will have no knowledge thereof. Behold! The crew are on the river on this day."

July 12   DAY SIXTEEN

Two Houses Fight   Horus and Sutekh

   Anyone born this day will be killed by a crocodile.
"It is the day (lost...) by Neith."

July 13   DAY SEVENTEEN

Second Arrival Day   Re

  Avoid *mehit*-fish today.

"It is the day of taking away Sobek's offering, namely taking the offering from his mouth."

Feast of the dead. Offerings given in the Necropolis.

July 14   DAY EIGHTEEN   ☉ ♙♙♙
Moon Day   Ahi

    Anything you see this day will be good.

"It is the day of increasing the majesty of Horus more than his brother, Sutekh, which the *naturu* did at the portal."

July 15   DAY NINETEEN   ☉🜂🜂🜂

Hear His Commands   Bring His Mother.

Burn sweetly scented incense on the fire for his followers in the Evening Boat and the Morning Boat Of The Sun, and for the *naturu*.

"A happy day in heaven in front of Re. Life! Prosperity! Health!

The *Paut Naturu* is in great festivity. It is the day of receiving (lost...) It is the day of going to (lost...) the *Heh* before *Babai*."

Festival of Nut and Re. Main festival of Thoth.

(*Note*: *Babai* is Sutekh is the guise of a baboon, attended by a pack of 77 black dogs who bit Horus when he was a child.)

THOTH

July 16   DAY TWENTY   ⊙ 𓎛𓎛𓎛𓎛

Offering Meat   Opener Of The Ways

Do not work this day.

"It is the day when the Great Ones, the followers of both Horus and Sutekh, take sides in the dispute."

July 17   DAY TWENTY-ONE   ☉♨♨♨

Apru's Day   Anubis

"Make offerings to Re's followers. Avoid bulls. Kill none, nor let any cross in front of you. It is a day to be cautious of bulls."

(Lost...)

July 18   DAY TWENTY-TWO   ☉𓂧𓂊𓂧𓂊𓂧
Passing Of Sopdut   Nai

   Eat no birds or fish today. Avoid heating or warming oil.

"Re calls every *natur* and *naturit* to him. They await his arrival. He takes them into his belly, and when they begin to move within him, he kills them. After doing so, he vomits them into the water. Their bodies become fish, which are not caught, and their souls become birds which fly up to heaven. (Lost...) on this day."

Sacred to Osiris.

July 19   DAY TWENTY-THREE   ☉ 𓂋𓂝𓂋𓂝𓂋𓂝

Last Quarter Day   Na-Ur

Do not burn incense on the fire of the *naturu* on this day. Do not kill any *inhy*-reptile, or any creature among the birds. Do not eat on this day. Avoid music and dancing. Do not listen to it or watch it. Those born today will not live. "It is the day of causing the heart of Apophis, the enemy of Re (Life! Prosperity! Health!) to suffer for what he has done against Re's children."

(*Note*: The *inhy*-reptile is a serpent who protects the dead,
so this is a prohibition against disturbing gravesites or tombs.)

THOTH

July 20   DAY TWENTY-FOUR   ☉𓀀𓀀
Darkness   Nekhbet

Those born today will die in honorable old age.
"The majesty of the *natur* Re sails peacefully in favorable winds (lost...) Behold!
His heart grows calm as he appears in the Evening Boat and then rises in the
Morning Boat."

July 21   DAY TWENTY-FIVE   ⊙◖◗◖◗◖
Departing   Shem
Do not leave your house or travel at the time of night on any roads.
"Sakhmet goes to the eastern district and drives back the confederates of Sutekh.
Any lion they approach passes away at once."

Sacred to Sakhmet. Mysteries of Osiris. Feast of Lights Of Isis.

(*Note*: There is evidence that this Festival is the true Festival Of Intoxication, and that the myth of
Sakhmet's threatened destruction of humankind is the basis for this festival. The Nile turns red with silt
as in the re-enactment of this flood of beer. This feast of intoxication is the ancient "October fest.")

July 22   DAY TWENTY-SIX   ☉ 𓂋𓏤𓂋𓏤𓂋𓏤

House Of Appearances   Ma'atef-f

Do nothing on this day.

"On this day Horus struggles with Sutekh. They grapple with each other in the form of men. They turn into ebony and spend three days and four nights this way. Then Isis let down a harpoon and it fell before her son Horus. She calls upon the harpoon, saying, "Loosen! Loosen from my son Horus!" Thereupon, the harpoon loosened from Horus. Another harpoon is let down, which falls in front of Sutekh. He cries out to it, saying, "Behold! I am her brother Sutekh." Then Isis calls out to this harpoon, "Be strong! Be strong!" Then Sutekh shouts to his sister many times, "Do you prefer the foreign man to a mother's brother?" Then she (lost…) evil (lost…) called on the harpoon, saying, "Loosen! Loosen! Behold! My brother of my mother!" Thereupon, the harpoon turned away from Sutekh. The opponents stand up as two men once more and they turn their backs on each other. Then the majesty of Horus becomes angry with his mother, and he turns on her like a panther. She flees before him."

Honors the battle between Horus and Sutekh.

July 23   DAY TWENTY-SEVEN   ☉⚚⚚⚚

Funerary Offerings   Khnum

Make a holiday. Avoid killing reptiles.

"There is peace between Horus and Sutekh."

Honors the peace between Horus and Sutekh.

July 24   DAY TWENTY-EIGHT   ☉⚕⚕⚕

Jubilee Of The Sky   Nut

    Anything you see this day will be good.

"The *naturu* are happy today when they see the children of Nut peaceful and content."

July 25   DAY TWENTY-NINE   ☉⌂⛭♊

Weakness   Utettef-f

Light no fires in your home. Burn no ointment. Stay in this night.
(Lost...)

Sky Feast of Re.

(*Note*: the ointment referred to is the fragrant oil that might be on someone's hands. The warning refers to
accidentally burning any that may have rubbed off onto the day's burnt offering.)

July 26   DAY THIRTY   ☉♨♨♨

Awaken   Horus Advocates For Him.

Anything you see this day will be good.

"Last Day.

House Of Re, House Of Osiris, House Of Horus."

Ritual day in the Houses Of Re, Of Osiris and Of Horus.

ADDITIONAL NOTES ON THE MONTH OF THUTHY:

PAOPY

Ptah is the *natur* of this month.

SECOND MONTH OF AKHET

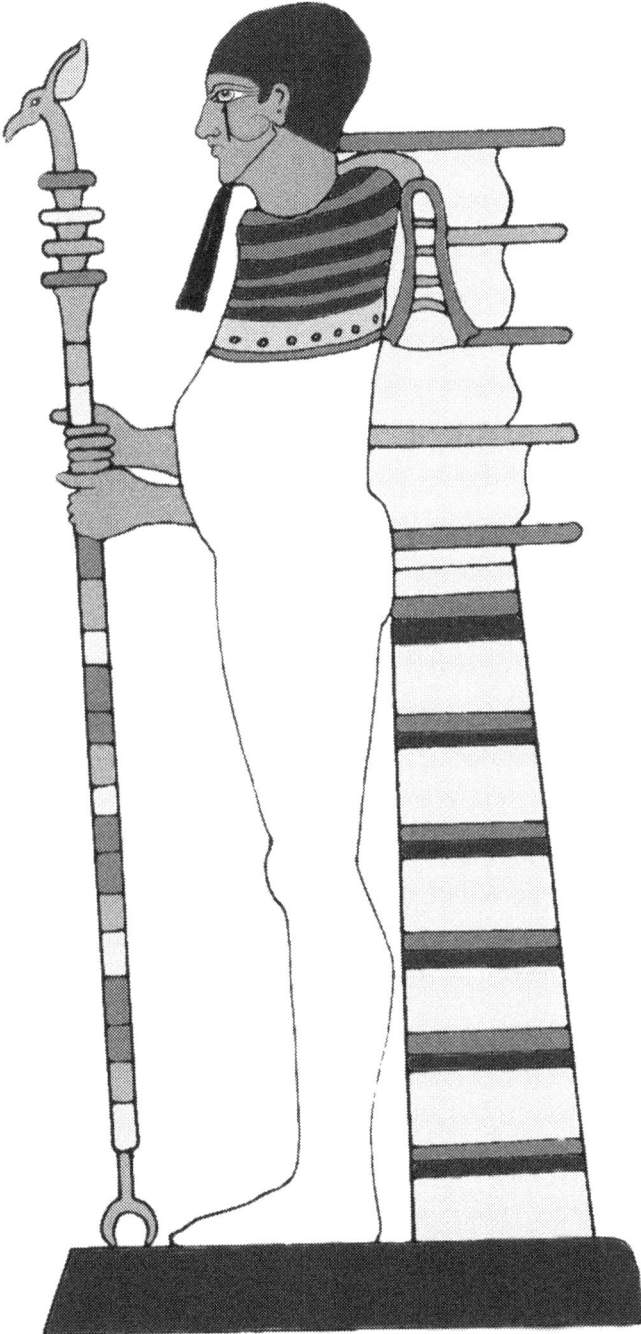

July 27   DAY ONE   ☉♅♅♅
New Month Day   Thoth
   (Lost...)

"Jubilation. The Great *Paut Naturu* is in celebration this day. On this day the
heritage of the Great Heir is established."

First day of Paopy. Sacred day of Re.

(*Note*: The Great Heir is Horus, who inherits the throne of Osiris.)

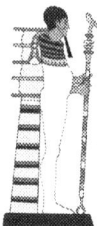

July 28   DAY TWO   (omission)
New Crescent Day   Horus

It is important that you listen on this day. Offer to all the *naturu*.
"The majesty of *Saut* (Sais) of Lower Egypt proceeds to his mother. She sees that he was suffering from his buttocks. Repetition of birth (lost...) great festivity."
Procession of Horus to the city of Neith.

July 29   DAY THREE   ☉⚬👤👤👤
Arrival Day   Osiris

   Anything you see will be good.
"Thoth is in the presence of Re in the inaccessible shrine. Re gives him the written order of the reconciliation of the *Wadjet* Eye. Hu and Sia are in the midst of his followers (lost...) in his manner."
"Thoth orders the Eye Of Horus healed."

(*Note*: Hu and Sia are the authority and intelligence of Re.)

PTAH

July 30   DAY FOUR   Isis
Zem Priests Emerge

   Those born today will die of a skin rash.
"It is the day of the emergence of Anubis to inspect the *wabet* for the protection of the body of the *natur* (Osiris.)"

July 31   DAY FIVE   ☉ 𓊪𓏤𓊪𓏤𓊪𓏤

Altar Offerings Day   Hapy

Those born this day will die making love. Do not leave your house by any roads this day. Do not make love.

"This is the day of offering before *Hedj-Hotpy* and *Montu*."

Feast of Osiris.

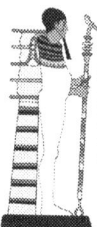

August 1   DAY SIX   ⊙⚱⚱⚱
Sixth Day   Star Of His Mother

Anyone born on this day will die intoxicated.

"It is a happy day for Re in heaven, and the *naturu* are calmed within his presence. The *Paut Naturu* exalts before the Lord Of The Universe."

Feast of Thoth, Opet, the marriage of Amon Re to his wife Amonet.

August 2　　　　　　DAY SEVEN　　　⊙⬭⬭⬭⬭⬭

First Quarter Day　　　　　　　　　　　　　　　　Qebsenuf

　　Those born today will die in a foreign land. Do nothing today.

"Today Re goes (lost...) to the countries, which he created in order to slay the children of rebellion. He returns (lost...) his neck and executes them before the *Paut Naturu*."

Monthly feast of Re.

August 3 DAY EIGHT

Main Emergence Ma'atef-f

Anything you see will be good.

(Lost...)

August 4   DAY NINE   ☉♌

Hidden One   He Does The Talking.

Those born today will die of old age.

"There is joy in the heart of Re (Lost...) His *Paut Naturu* is in celebration. All Re's enemies are overthrown."

Jubilation of the heart of Re.

August 5   DAY TEN   ☉𓏏𓏏𓏏

He Who Protects His Royal Name   He Makes A Name Himself.
   (Lost...)

"The majesty of Bastet, Lady of *Ankh-towe* (a city near Memphis) emerges, and his majesty Re of *Innu* inquires about her payment of tribute to the august tree. It is pleasing to his followers."

Procession of Bastet. The birth of Nut.

(*Note*: this may be the sacred *erica* tree of Osiris; the dawn tree which Re climbs like a cat, or the tree in Memphis with names of pharaohs on its leaves, or the World Tree.)

August 6   DAY ELEVEN   ☉𒀭𒀭𒀭

Great Lady Protector   Sakhmet
   All is good this day.
"This day they repair the front piece on the bow of the Sun Boat. Life!
Prosperity! Health! Before the august (lost...) which is established behind him."
Monthly feast of Re.

August 7 · · · · · · · DAY TWELVE

Making Love · · · · · · · Bring The Advocate.

Do nothing this day.

"Today he who rebels his lord raises his head in hostility. His words drown out the speech of Sutekh, son of Nut. The rebel's head is removed for having conspired against his lord."

Birth of Hathor.

August 8　　　　　　　　　DAY THIRTEEN　　　　　　⊙♕
Approach of Re　　　　　　　　　　　　　　　　　　　　　　Re
(Lost...)
"The hearts of the *naturu* are pleased by a feast and by honoring their lord,
he who defeated the enemy so they will no longer exist."
Satisfying the hearts of the Paut Naturu.

August 9   DAY FOURTEEN

Progress Of The Ba   Consider The Ba.

Make offering to your *naturu*. Pacify the spirits.

"The majesty of Horus receives the White Crown. The *Paut Naturu* of his followers rejoice."

Horus receives the White Crown.

August 10   DAY FIFTEEN   ☉🜚🝢🝣🝢🝣

Half Month Day   Amauai

Do not leave your house at night. If anyone sees them, he will pass away at once. "The majesty of Re goes out at nightfall with his followers."

August 11   DAY SIXTEEN   ☉♌︎

Two Houses Fight   Horus and Sutekh

   Anything you see will be good.

"The *naturu* attending the feast of Osiris are joyous. The hearts of the *Paut Naturu* are pleased."

Feast of Osiris.

August 12　　　　　　DAY SEVENTEEN　　　　⊙♌♌♌
Second Arrival Day　　　　　　　　　　　　　　　　Re

　It is important to offer bread and beer and to burn incense this day. It is necessary to make an invocation offering to the spirits so that your words will be heard by your sky *naturu*.

"Smelling (lost...) on this day by the Great *Paut Naturu* and the Lesser *Paut Naturu* who comes out of Nun."

August 13   DAY EIGHTEEN   ☉ 𓂋𓂽𓂋𓂽𓂋𓂽

Moon Day   Ahi.

Do nothing this day.

"On this day Anubis inspects the embalming tent, while performing the transformation into lizards in the sight of men. Anubis found all things being ready to care for the burial. Then he started to weep. He repeated the inspection while still weeping. They begin to weep aloud. They place their hands upon their heads, both the *naturu* and the *naturitu*."

Ceremony of Transformation by Anubis. Mummification of Osiris.

August 14   DAY NINETEEN   ☉♀♀♀

Hear His Commands   Bring His Mother.
   (Lost...)

"Nun goes out to set the Noble One in his place, and to give redress to the *naturu* who are in the presence of the Noble One."

Ceremony of raising the sacred Djed pillar.

August 15   DAY TWENTY   ☉⤸⤹⤸⤹⤸⤹

Offering Meat   Opener Of The Ways

(Lost...)

"It is the day of giving payment in the presence of Re, and the manner in which Thoth makes an example out of defeating the rebels of their lord. They are carried off by Sutekh, son of Nut, and they will be underneath. So say the *naturu*."

August 16   DAY TWENTY-ONE   ☉𓃀𓂝𓃀𓂝𓊌

Apru's Day   Anubis

(Lost...)

"The *naturit* Neith of Upper Egypt goes before the presence of Re. May he live and be prosperous! While appeasing and praising Neith, her eyes guide Thoth."

Neith emerges before Ra.

August 17   DAY TWENTY-TWO   ☉ 𓃻𓃻𓃻𓃻

Passing Of Sopdut   Nai

   Do not bathe this day.

"It is the day they cut the tongue of Sobek's enemy."

August 18
DAY TWENTY-THREE   ☉☥𓂋𓂋
Last Quarter Day   Na-Ur
  A crocodile will kill anyone born this day. (Lost...)

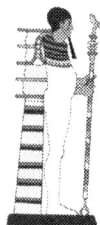

August 19   DAY TWENTY-FOUR   ☉ 𓆗𓆗𓆗
Darkness   Nekhbet

   Do not go out of your house in any wind until Re sets.
"On this day the executioners of *Saut* go looking for the children of rebellion,
when he is in the ocean. If any lion glances at them he will die immediately."

August 20   DAY TWENTY-FIVE   ☉ 𓂀𓂀𓂀

Departing   Shem

Do not leave your house or travel on any roads.

"This is the day they find the children of rebellion wrapped in a mat, on their sides. (Lost...) in his charge. (Lost...) if a lion looks for the *naturu* today, he will suffer from the trampling of a bull and die."

(*Note*: this is an older form of burial, with the rebels corpses hung alongside Re's Boat.)

August 21   DAY TWENTY-SIX   ☉ 𓂀𓏤𓂀𓏤𓂀𓏤

House Of Appearance   Ma'atef-f

Build no house foundations. Put no ships in the shipyard. Do not work today. "It is the day for opening and resealing the windows in the palace at the House Of Osiris."

August 22   DAY TWENTY-SEVEN   ☉𓂀𓂀𓂀
Funerary Offerings   Khnumu

   Make a holiday. Avoid killing reptiles. Do not go out. Do not give your back
to any work. Anyone born on this day will die from snakebite. (Lost...)
                    Lighting the fires of Neith.

August 23   DAY TWENTY-EIGHT   ☉♀♀♀

Jubilee Of The Sky   Nut

Anything you see this day will be good. (Lost...)

August 24
DAY TWENTY-NINE
⊙♀♀♀

Weakness
Utettef-f

Anyone born this day will die honored by the people.
(Lost...)

August 25   DAY THIRTY   ☉⚏
Awaken   Horus Advocates For Him.
   (Lost...)

"Last day. Found missing (lost...) by Nun, father of the *naturu*. The land is joyous on this day. House Of Re. House Of Osiris. House Of Horus."

Sky Feast of Re. Feasts of Osiris and Horus.

ADDITIONAL NOTES ON THE MONTH OF PAOPY:

PTAH

HATHYS

Hathor is the *naturit* of this month.

THIRD MONTH OF AKHET

August 26   DAY ONE   ☉⚱⚱⚱

New Month Day   Thoth
  (Lost...)

"Feast of Hathor, Lady Of Heaven. (Lost...) *naturu* (lost...) Lady of all the *naturitu*."
Month of Hathys begins. Feast of Hathor. Feast of Re.

HATHOR

August 27   DAY TWO   ☉♀♀♀

New Crescent Day   Horus

     Anything you see will be good.

"Return of the *Wadjet* Eye from *Dop* (pre-dynastic capital) In order to relate (lost...)"

August 28   DAY THREE   ⊙♦♦♦
Arrival Day   Osiris
   Anything you see will be good.
"He is received by the noble *naturu*."

August 29   DAY FOUR

Zem Priests Emerge   Isis

Anyone who sails this day will see his house destroyed. "The Earth trembles under Nun."

August 30   DAY FIVE   ☉ 𓂀𓃾𓂀𓃾𓂀
Altar Offerings Day   Hapy

Put out the fires in your house. Avoid gazing at fire.
"This is the day the *naturu* are blamed (lost...) by the majesty of these *naturu*."
Honor Hathor.

August 31 DAY SIX

Sixth Day Star Of His Mother

(Lost...)

"The Encouragement of the *naturu* of the Dual Dimensions on this day (lost...) Encouragement of (lost...) the whole land."

Feast of the naturu of the black mud of Egypt.

(*Note*: The "encouragement" is an command by Pharaoh to his soldiers, urging them on to fight, given here to the followers of Horus and Sutekh.)

September 1   DAY SEVEN   ⊙♨♨♨

First Quarter Day   Qebsenuf

  Anything you see will be good.

(Lost...)

Monthly feast of Re.

September 2   DAY EIGHT   (omission)

Main Emergence   Ma'atef-f

(Lost...)

"Isis emerges. Her heart is pleased on this day. Horus's heritage is established."

HATHOR

September 3   DAY NINE   ☉ 𓂀𓂀𓂀

Hidden One   He Does The Talking.

  Do not leave your house by any road. Do not let light fall upon your face until Re sets.

"It is the day of blaming the Great Ones who are in his presence."

Isis emerges.

HATHOR

September 4   DAY TEN

He Who Protects His Royal Name   He Makes A Name Himself.

   (Lost...) "There is great rejoicing in heaven. The crews of Re are at peace. His *Paut Naturu* shouts with pleasure at seeing those working in the fields."

HATHOR

September 5   DAY ELEVEN   ☉♀♀♀

Great Lady Protector   Sakhmet

 All is good this day. Anything you see will be good.

(Lost...)

Monthly feast of Re.

HATHOR

September 6   DAY TWELVE   (omission)
Making Love   Bring The Advocate.
  (Lost...)

"The appeasement of the *naturu's* hearts wherever they are. The *Wadjet* Eye is on the head of Re. Fixing (lost...) for the *naturu*, raising those who are upon their thrones."

Osiris goes out of Ibtu. Purification of the naturu's and naturitu's hearts.
Feast of Hapy. Offerings are given to the Nile this day.

HATHOR

September 7   DAY THIRTEEN   ☉ 𓂧𓏏𓂧𓏏𓂧𓏏

Approach of Re   Re

(Lost...) "The ferryman on the river is cut into pieces on this day, for not fer-
rying over the confederates of Sutekh. (Lost...) any (lost...) against the Boat Of
Osiris, which was sailing upstream to *Ibtu*, the great city of Osiris. Behold! He
is transformed into a little old person carried in the arms of his nurse. (Lost...)
giving gold as a reward to *Inty* as a fare, saying, 'Please ferry me over to the
West.' Then he (lost...) takes it from him. Behold! The confederates were following like a swarm of reptiles. Thereupon he recognizes these, while Sutekh enters
into the embalming booth to see the *natur's* limbs. When they become fresh,
Sutekh came (lost...) as an enemy on the water. The rebels following him are
transformed into small cattle. Horus and his followers slaughter the small cattle. They divide them among the crew. An offering was made of the tongues
of the enemy of *Inty*, in order to fix firmly the gold in the House Of
Inty forever. One was awed at the small cattle in the West. One was awed
at the transforming of small cattle into flocks of birds, until this day."

Hapy is created.

HATHOR

September 8   DAY FOURTEEN   ☉𝄐𝄐𝄐

Progress Of The Ba   Consider The Ba.

Do nothing this day. Anyone born this day will die of (lost...)

"The hearts of the *naturu* are saddened because of what was done by the enemy of *Inty*."

Jubilation of the dead.

September 9   DAY FIFTEEN   ☉𓂀𓂀𓂀
Half Month Day   Amauai
   (Lost...)

"Consideration by *Banob-Tet* (Osiris as the *natur* of fertility, or the Ram of Mendes) (lost...) in the sacred House Of Life."

   Fertility of Min. A day of offerings to Min, especially by husbands wishing for sons.

September 10   DAY SIXTEEN   ☉♊

Two Houses Fight   Horus and Sutekh

   A happy day without end.

"The Great Ones appear in *Shmun*. Bringing of the ibis (lost...) establishing (lost...) in *Shmun*, a joyous day in infinity and eternity."

Day of the appearance of the Eight Primordials.

(*Note*: *Shmun* is *Khemennu*, Thoth's town or the "City Of The Eight," was also called *Per Tehuty*, and Hermopolis by the Greeks. Today it is called *El-Ashmunein*. The Eight Primordials are the four paired*naturu* of the creation story of Thoth's priests.)

September 11   DAY SEVENTEEN   ☉♌

Second Arrival Day   Re
  (Lost...)

"The Great *Paut Naturu* lands at *Ibtu*. Isis and Lady Of The House weep and wail loudly for Osiris in *Saut*. It is heard in *Ibtu*."

Lamentation of Isis and Lady Of The House for Osiris.

September 12   DAY EIGHTEEN   ☉𓂋𓏤𓂋𓏤𓂋𓏤

Moon Day   Ahi

If making a journey, do not go near roads.

"There is strife by Sutekh and Isis, the children of Geb. (Lost...)"

Feast of Hathor. The statue of the naturit is taken on a boating procession to the mortuary complexes, to visit the pharaoh's tomb.

September 13   DAY NINETEEN   ☉❧❧❧❧❧

Hear His Commands   Bring His Mother.

Do not sail north or south. So not sail boats this day.
"The children of the storm of Apophis (lost...)"

HATHOR

September 14   DAY TWENTY   ☉ 𓂋𓏤𓂋𓏤𓂋
Offering Meat   Opener Of The Ways.

Those born this day will perish during a year of pestilence.
"The emergence of Bastet, Lady of *Ankh-towe*, before Re. She is greatly angered.
The *naturu* could not stand near her. (Bastet has become a Great Flame.)"
Bastet appears before Re.

September 15   DAY TWENTY-ONE   ☉👁👁👁

Apru's Day   Anubis
  (Lost...)

"The feast of Shu, son of Re. It is the day of Neith in the Evening Boat Of The Sun."

Feast of Ma'at.

September 16   DAY TWENTY-TWO   (omission)
Passing Of Sopdut   Nai
  (Lost...)

"When *Ma'at* is summoned before Re, the *naturu* raise her up in order to see him. A Uraeus is placed upon her and another below her, being fixed at the front of the Evening Boat Of The Sun."

(*Note*: In every House Of The *Natur,* a figure of *Ma'at* is presented to the *natur* by the priest or supplicant to the *naturu* during rituals.)

HATHOR

September 17   DAY TWENTY-THREE   ☉𓂋𓂦𓂋𓂦

Last Quarter Day   Na-Ur

   Those who were born this day will not survive.

"Nun drags (lost...) them from the flames by the hands. Behold! The majesty of these *naturu* who judge in that great place (lost...) on the river."

The dispute between Horus and Sutekh judged by Re.

September 18   DAY TWENTY-FOUR   ☉♈♈♈

Darkness   Nekhbet

(Lost...)

'Isis emerges. Her heart is happy and Lady Of The House is joyous. When they see Osiris (lost...) heart. He has given his throne to his son Horus in the presence of Re."

Isis emerges.

HATHOR

September 19   DAY TWENTY-FIVE   ☉♊♊♊

Departing   Shem

Anything you see will be pleasing to the *naturu*.

(Lost...)

September 20   DAY TWENTY-SIX   ☉♌♌♌

House Of Appearances   Ma'atef-f
  (Lost...)

"Raising the *Djed* of Re in the heaven and land of *Innu* at the time of uproar, and reconciliation of the Two Lords causes the land to be a peace. The Black Land is granted to Horus and the Red Land to Sutekh. Thoth emerges in order to judge in the presence of Re."

The Black Land is given to Horus, the Red Land to Sutekh.

HATHOR

September 21   DAY TWENTY-SEVEN   ☉♀♙♙♙

Funerary Offerings   Khnumu

"The judgment between Sutekh and Horus stops the hostility. They hunt down the followers of the two *natury*, and put an end to the tumult. It satisfies the Two Lords and causes the two doors to open."

The Autumn Equinox.

September 22   DAY TWENTY-EIGHT   ☉𝍄𝍄𝍄

Jubilee Of The Sky   Nut

Anything you see this day will be good.

"All the *naturu* are jubilant because the will is written for Horus, son of Osiris, to appease Osiris in the *Heh*. The land is joyous and the *naturu* are pleased."

Horus is crowned King. The appearance before Ptah.

September 23   DAY TWENTY-NINE   ☉⦚⦚⦚

Weakness   Utettef-f

  (Lost...)

"The emergence of the Three Noble Ladies who are in the *Tanent* Sanctuary in the presence of Ptah, beautiful of face, while they give praise to Re, he who belongs to the throne of *Ma'at* of the Houses Of The *Naturitu*. For giving the White Crown to Horus and the Red Crown to Sutekh, their hearts are pleased."

September 24 DAY THIRTY ☉♀♀♀

Awaken Horus Advocates For Him.

Anything you see will be good.

"Last day. House Of Re, House Of Osiris, House Of Horus."

Feast of the Noble Ladies. Sky Feast.

ADDITIONAL NOTES ON THE MONTH OF HATHYS:

CHOIACH

September 25 to October 24

Sekhtet is the *naturit* of this month.

FINAL MONTH OF AKHET

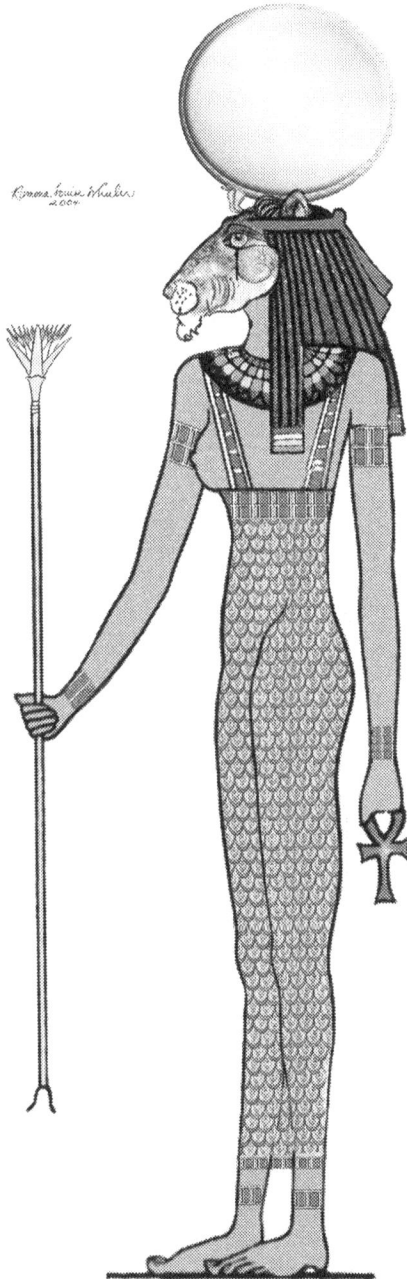

September 25   DAY ONE   ☉♔♔♔

New Month Day   Thoth
 (Lost...)

"The Great *Paut Naturu* and the Lesser *Paut Naturu* go to appease the majesty of Nun in the cavern. The majesty of Thoth orders Sia and his followers (lost...) saying, 'A copy of the command of the majesty of Re is brought to you. Re is joyful in his beauty. His *Paut Naturu* is in celebration. Every lion and all *inhy*-reptiles, the *naturu, naturitu*, spirits, dead and those who came into being in the primordial age, their form is in every one of you.'"

Month of Choiach begins. Feast of Re and Sakhmet.

SEKHMET

September 26   DAY TWO   ☉⚕⚕⚕

New Crescent Day   Horus

   Anything you see will be good.

"The *naturu* and *naturitu* are joyous. Heaven and Earth are happy."

SEKHMET

September 27　　　　　　DAY THREE　　　　　⊙ ☧☧☧☧☧

Arrival Day　　　　　　　　　　　　　　　　　　　　　Osiris

　Do nothing this day. Those born this day will die of his ears.

"It is the day of smashing the ears of *Bata* within his own inaccessible Houses Of Life."

(*Note*: Offering-bread had molded ears so the *naturu* could hear prayers.

In the Old Kingdom, there was a practice of smashing ears off sculptured portrait heads.)

SEKHMET

September 28   DAY FOUR   ☉♀♀♀

Zem Priests Emerge   Isis

Using all that is required, perform Sobek's rituals in your home and in his House Of Life.

"It will please the hearts of the *naturu* on this day."

Feast of Sobek. Sacred crocodiles are honored this day.

SEKHMET

September 29   DAY FIVE   ☉♌♌♌
Altar Offerings Day   Hapy
   (Lost...)

"The emergence of *Khentet-abet* (Hathor) in the presence of the Great Ones (Horus and Sutekh) in *Kher-Aaha*. Life, stability and welfare are given to her and the *Paut Naturu*.

The *naturu* of the *Kher-Aaha* and the majesty of Hapy, father of the *naturu*, are joyous this day."

Procession of Hathor.

(*Note: Khentet-Abet* is Hathor. *Kher-Aaha* is the scene of the battles of Horus and Sutekh.)

SEKHMET

September 30

DAY SIX

Sixth Day

Star Of His Mother

Do not go out on this day.

"The Sun Boat of Re is established in order to overthrow his foes from one moment to another this day."

SEKHMET

October 1   DAY SEVEN

First Quarter Day   Qebsenuf

Do not eat or taste *mehit* fish this day.

"It is the day of (lost...) wind. (Lost...) death in (lost...) he will turn into a fish."

Feast of Sorqet. Feast of Thoth.

SEKHMET

October 2 DAY EIGHT

Main Emergence

Ma'atef-f

Anything you see will be good.

(Lost...)

Monthly feast of Re.

SEKHMET

October 3   DAY NINE   ☉♦♦♦

Hidden One   He Does The Talking.
   (Lost...)

"It is the day of action by Thoth. Re speaks in the presence of the Great Ones. Then together with Thoth, these *naturu* cause the enemy of Sutekh to kill himself in his sanctuary. It is this that has been done by the executioners of (lost...) until this day."

SEKHMET

October 4   DAY TEN   ☉♨♨♨

He Who Protects His Royal Name   He Makes A Name Himself.

Those born this day will die in old age, while beer enters into his mouth, face and eyes. Those born on this day will die in old age, choking to death swallowing beer.

(Lost...)

SEKHMET

October 5   DAY ELEVEN   ☉♈♈♈

Great Lady Protector   Sakhmet

(omission) Feast of Osiris in *Ibtu* in the Great *Neshmet* (the sacred boat of Re and Osiris) on this day.

"The dead are joyous."

Feast of Osiris in Ibtu.

SEKHMET

October 6

DAY TWELVE

⊙ 𓈖𓏏𓈖𓏏𓈖𓏏

Making Love

Bring The Advocate.

Make offerings to the *Bennu*-phoenix in your home. Stay off windy roads this day.

"It is the day of transformation into the *Bennu*-phoenix."

Transformation of the Bennu Bird (Re).

SEKHMET

October 7   DAY THIRTEEN   ☉♀♀♀

Approach of Re   Re

Make this a sacred day in your house. Make a feast in your house on this day. "The emergence of the White One of Heaven (Hathor). Their hearts are pleased for her in the presence of Re. The *Paut Naturu* is in celebration."

Procession of Hathor and the Paut Naturu.

SEKHMET

October 8
DAY FOURTEEN ⊙♔♔♔

Progress Of The Ba
(Lost...)

Consider The Ba.

"Lady Of The House and *Tait* come from the House Of The *Natur* of the *Benben* on this day. They present things to Neith. Their hearts are happy."

Feast of naturu and naturitu and Fate. Emergence of the transformed Bennu-phoenix.

(*Note*: *Tait* is Lady Of The House as the *Naturit* of weaving. Lady Of The House provided the role model for a woman's responsibilities as household manager.)

SEKHMET

October 9   DAY FIFTEEN   (Lost...)
Half Month Day   Amauai
(Lost...) Feast of Sakhmet and Bastet.
Feast of Sakhmet, Bastet and Re.

SEKHMET

October 10

DAY SIXTEEN

(Lost...)

Two Houses Fight

Horus and Sutekh

(Day lost to papyrus damage.)

SEKHMET

October 11   DAY SEVENTEEN   ☉𓂝𓂝𓂝

Second Arrival Day   Re

Stay home during the middle part of the day.

"The people and the *naturu* judge the words of the crew in *Innu* when Horus arrives in *Kher-Aaha*."

> *Feast of the judging of the crew of the Sun Boat. Sacred day of Hathor.*

SEKHMET

October 12   DAY EIGHTEEN   ⊙𓂋𓂋𓂋

Moon Day   Ahi

  (Lost...)

"It is the day of the overthrowing of the *naturu's* boat on this day."

SEKHMET

October 13   DAY NINETEEN   ☉ 𓂀𓂀𓂀𓂀

Hear His Commands   Bring His Mother.

Drink no wine. Do not partake of bread or beer. Drink only the water of grapes until sunset.

"Offerings are presented in the *Hewit*-desert. Ointment is made for Osiris in the hall of embalming."

SEKHMET

October 14   DAY TWENTY   ☉ 𓂋𓏤𓂋𓏤𓂋𓏤

Offering Meat   Opener Of The Ways

Stay off roads. Wear no ointments (perfumed oils.) Stay in when the Sun is at noon.

"It is the day of looking in the direction of the *Akhet* Eye Of Horus."

SEKHMET

October 15 DAY TWENTY-ONE

Apru's Day Anubis

  Do not leave your house during the hours of daylight.

"This is the day of the emergence of the Great Ones to look for the *Akhet* Eye Of Horus."

Ritual of raising the Djed pillar.

October 16   DAY TWENTY-TWO   ☉ ♁♁♁

Passing Of Sopdut   Nai

   Anything you see will be good. (Lost...)

Feast of plowing the Earth.

SEKHMET

October 17   DAY TWENTY-THREE

Last Quarter Day   Na-Ur

Do not go out during the hours of darkness. Should a lion see you if you go out this night, he will kill you.

"They (lost...) in order to defeat (lost...) Horus, who is the savior of his father."

SEKHMET

October 18   DAY TWENTY-FOUR   (Lost...)

Darkness   Nekhbet

(Day lost to papyrus damage.)

SEKHMET

October 19   DAY TWENTY-FIVE   (Lost...)

Departing   Shem

(Day lost to papyrus damage.)

SEKHMET

October 20   DAY TWENTY-SIX   ☉☖☖☖

House Of Appearance   Ma'atef-f

(Lost...)

"Thoth raised the nobles to an advanced position in the city of Sakhmet (Letopolis.) (Lost...)"

SEKHMET

October 21   DAY TWENTY-SEVEN   ⊙🦆🧍🦆⚱️

Funerary Offerings   Khnumu

Anything you see in the daylight will be good. Do not go out during the hours of darkness this day.

(Lost...)

Feast of Isis seeking Osiris's body.

SEKHMET

October 22

DAY TWENTY-EIGHT

Jubilee Of The Sky

Nut

Eat no *mehit*-fish this day. Do not use it as an offering.
"It is the day of the emergence of the *ba-mehit*-fish, which is in the House Of Osiris, its form being the *iten*-fish."

Feast of the loss of Osiris by Isis.

SEKHMET

October 23   DAY TWENTY-NINE   ☉〰〰〰
Weakness   Utettef-f

Avoid the scent of fish while throwing flame into the water from what is offered. Eat no *mehit*-fish. Do not let one touch you, or take one into your hands. (Lost...)

Feast of rejoicing that Isis has found the body of Osiris.

SEKHMET

October 24   DAY THIRTY   ☉♦♦♦

Awaken   Horus Advocates For Him.

Anything you see will please hearts of the *naturu* this day. Make offerings to them and their followers, and make invocation offerings to the spirits. Offer to the dead. Give food in accordance to the List.

It is a day of pleasure for the Great *Paut Naturu.*
"House Of Re. House Of Osiris. House Of Horus."

Feast of the Paut of Re. Feast of Osiris and Horus. Offerings for the ka.

SEKHMET

ADDITIONAL NOTES ON THE MONTH OF CHOIACH:

SEKHMET

TYBY

Min is the *natur* of this month.

FIRST MONTH OF PORET

October 25   DAY ONE   ☉⫩⫩⫩

New Month Day   Thoth

Offer twice the usual amount. Give the gifts of *Hekenu*. Anything you see will be good.

"Double the offerings and bestow the gifts of *Hekenu* to the *naturu* who attend Ptah in the *Tanent* shrines of the *naturu* and *naturitu*, protectors of Re and his followers and of the (lost...) of Ptah-Sokar, Sakhmet the Great, Nofertum and Horus Of The Two Horizons, *Mahes* (a lioness-headed form of Sakhmet,) Bastet the Great Fire (lost...) propitiating the *Wadjet* Eye."

The month of Tyby begins. Feast of Re. Feast of Bastet. The Heb-Sed (Jubilee) Festival.

(*Note*: The word *Heb* means "Festival," and *Sed* means "cloth," as well as "tail." During this festival the King had to run around the circumference of the House Of Life (temple) inner court, carrying ritual objects in his hands that performed his rejuvenation during his race. This feast took place every three years, with an even grander version occurring at a Pharaoh's Thirtieth Year Jubilee.)

MIN

October 26   DAY TWO   (Lost...)
New Crescent Day   Horus
(Day lost to papyrus damage.)

MIN

October 27   DAY THREE   (Lost...)
Arrival Day   Osiris
  Light no fires to Re or in his presence.
(Lost...)

October 28   DAY FOUR   ☉♀♀♀

Zem Priests Emerge   Isis

Those born this day will die in old age among his family. He will spend a long lifetime and will be received by his father. (He will be justified.) Anything you see will be good.

(Lost...)

October 29   DAY FIVE   ☉☽♌︎♎︎♌︎♎︎

Altar Offerings Day   Hapy

"It is the day of Sakhmet placing the flame before the Great Ones who preside in the sanctuary of Lower Egypt. She is fierce in her manifestions because of her confinement in the sanctuary by *Ma'at*, Ptah, Thoth, Hu and Sia." (Lost...)

October 30   DAY SIX   ☉♊♊♊

Sixth Day   Star Of His Mother

Offer twice the Horus Of The Two Horizons offerings to the *naturu*. Offerings must be doubled. Repeat the food offerings of him who dwells in the Holy Place and return the food of the noble *Khenty-arty* (Horus.) (Lost...)

Feast of clothing Anubis.

October 31   DAY SEVEN   ⊙ 𓂋𓏤𓂋𓏤𓂋𓏤

First Quarter Day   Qebsenuf

Do not make love with anyone in the presence of the Great Flame. (Lost...)

Feast of Sakhmet and the purifying of the flame.

November 1   DAY EIGHT   ☉♨♨♨

Main Emergence   Ma'atef-f

   Anything you see will be good.

(Lost...)

Monthly feast of Re.

November 2   DAY NINE   ⊙♨

Hidden One   He Does The Talking.

Repeat offerings using *Paut* cakes, to please the *naturu* and spirits.

"The *naturu* are pleased with the offerings of Sakhmet this day."

Feast of Sakhmet.

(*Note*: *Paut* cake is any special kind of dough prepared for offering.)

November 3   DAY TEN   ☉⟰⟱⟰⟱⟰⟱

He Who Protects His Royal Name   He Makes A Name Himself.

   Do not burn papyrus this day.

"It is the day of the emergence of Horus and the Flame."

MIN

November 4   DAY ELEVEN   ☉𝋛𝋛𝋛𝋛𝋛

Great Lady Protector   Sakhmet
  Do not go near flame this day.
(Lost...)

November 5

DAY TWELVE

Making Love

Bring The Advocate.

　Do not go near any dogs this day.
"It is the day of answering the speech of Sakhmet."

Monthly feast of Re.

November 6　　　　　　DAY THIRTEEN　　　　　⊙⚍⚍
Approach of Re　　　　　　　　　　　　　　　　　　Re
(Lost...)

"It is the day of prolonging the life and bringing about acts of benevolence from the *naturit Ma'at* in the House Of The *Naturu*."

Feast of Hathor and Sakhmet. Day of prolonging life and the goodness of Ma'at.

November 7   DAY FOURTEEN   ☉⌂⥯⌂⥯⌂⥯

Progress Of The Ba   Consider The Ba.

   Avoid singers and chanting this day.

"This is the day Isis and Lady Of The House weep. This is the day they mourn Osiris in the House Of Osiris (Busiris) remembering what they had seen."

November 8   DAY FIFTEEN   ☉ 👁

Half Month Day   Amauai

   Anything you see will be good.

"It is the day Nun goes through the cave to that place where the *naturu* are (lost...) in darkness."

November 9　　　　　　　　DAY SIXTEEN　　　　　　⊙♌♌♌

Two Houses Fight　　　　　　　　　　　　　　　Horus and Sutekh

"This is the day of the emergence of Shu in order to count the crew of the Evening Boat Of The Sun."

November 10   DAY SEVENTEEN   ⊙ 𓈖𓏏𓈖𓏏𓈖𓏏

Second Arrival Day   Re

Do not wash yourself with water on this day.

"It is the day Nun emerges into the place where the *naturu* are. Those who are above and below come into being. The land is still in darkness."

(*Note*: this is the day the *naturu* are created. The Earth has yet to be created and the cosmos is in a state of watery chaos. Nun is the primeval water from which the cosmos arose and upon which it rests.)

November 11   DAY EIGHTEEN   ⊙⚵⚵⚵
Moon Day   Ahi

This day is a holiday in The Mouth Of The Far Horizon.
"The *naturu* emerge from *Ibtu*."

The naturu leave Ibtu for Mouth Of The Far Horizon.

(*Note*: The Mouth Of The Far Horizon is the region in the western horizon where the Sun sets. It is
represented by the mouth of Nut swallowing the setting Sun. This is the beginning of the night journey of
Re and this is the first port of the dead on their journey to the Next Life.)

MIN

November 12   DAY NINETEEN   ☉⌂⇄⌂⇄⌂⇄

Hear His Commands   Bring His Mother.

Those who are afflicted on this day, and do not mend before the day ends, will never recover.

"The Great *naturu* are in heaven on this day and mixed with the pestilence of the year. There are many deaths."

November 13   DAY TWENTY   ☉𝄐𝄐𝄐

Offering Meat   Opener Of The Ways

   Do nothing this day. Be ware of crossing over land. Do not cross land until Re sets.

"This day Bastet emerges to protect the Dual Dimensions and to care for him who is in darkness."

Bastet leaves Bubastis to guard the Dual Dimensions.

November 14   DAY TWENTY-ONE   ☉♊♊♊

Apru's Day   Anubis

Make spirit (*aabt*) offerings to the followers of Re on this day.
"Bastet guides the Dual Dimensions."

Feast for the followers of Re.

(*Note*: *aabt* are the funeral or sacrifical offerings.)

November 15   DAY TWENTY-TWO   ☉⚱⚱⚱

Passing Of Sopdut   Nai

Anything you see will be good.

(Lost...)

November 16   DAY TWENTY-THREE   ☉𓋹𓋹𓋹

Last Quarter Day   Na-Ur

  Those born today will die rich in everything at an old age.
(Lost...)

Feast of Neith.

November 17   DAY TWENTY-FOUR   ☉♦♦♦

Darkness   Nekhbet

   There is joy in both heaven and Earth.

"Everything is put behind him in the presence of the *Paut Naturu* on the occasion of being loyal to the executioners of Re. There is happiness in heaven and on Earth this day."

November 18   DAY TWENTY-FIVE   (omission)
Departing   Shem

Do not drink milk. Eat and drink honey.

"On this day the Great Divine Cow is brought before the presence of Re."

(*Note*: Hathor's role as *Meh-Urt*, who gave birth to the Sun each morning. Milk was offered to her on this day, and used in ritual bathing to purify before ceremonies in the House Of The *Natur*.

MIN

November 19   DAY TWENTY-SIX   ☉ 𓂋𓏤𓂋𓏤𓂋𓏤

House Of Appearances   Ma'atef-f

Do not go out on this day until Re sets, once the offerings are diminished in the House Of Osiris and while they are put on Earth towards heaven. "There will be much blame for it."

November 20   DAY TWENTY-SEVEN   ☉⚚⚚

Funerary Offerings   Khnumu
  "Great festivity in (lost...) *Hefau (*Apophis.)"
(Lost...)

November 21   DAY TWENTY-EIGHT   ☉👥👥👥

Jubilee Of The Sky   Nut

All the land is in festivity. Make a holiday at home.

"Thoth takes a solemn oath in *Khemennu* (Town Of The Eight) and the Noble One emerges. The land is in celebration."

Feast of Thoth's oath.

November 22   DAY TWENTY-NINE ☉♨

Weakness   Utettef-f

Anything you see will be good.

"Appearance in the sight of Hu. Thoth sends a command southward, by Bastet and Sakhmet The Great, to guide the Dual Dimensions. The *naturu* are happy."

Sky feast.

November 23   DAY THIRTY   ☉♌♌♌

Awaken   Horus Advocates For Him.

Forget no one when you offer incense in the Houses Of Re and Osiris and Horus. Do not forget any of them whle incense is on the fire, according to the list on this day.

"Last day. The crossing over in the presence of Nun from the House Of Hapy, father of the *naturu* and the *Paut Naturu* lords of *Kher-Aaba*. House Of Re. House Of Osiris. House Of Horus."

Feast in the House Of Life of Hapy.

Additional Notes on the Month of Tyby:

MIN

MENCHIR

November 24 to December 23

Rekeh-Ur is the *naturit* of this month.
SECOND MONTH OF PORET

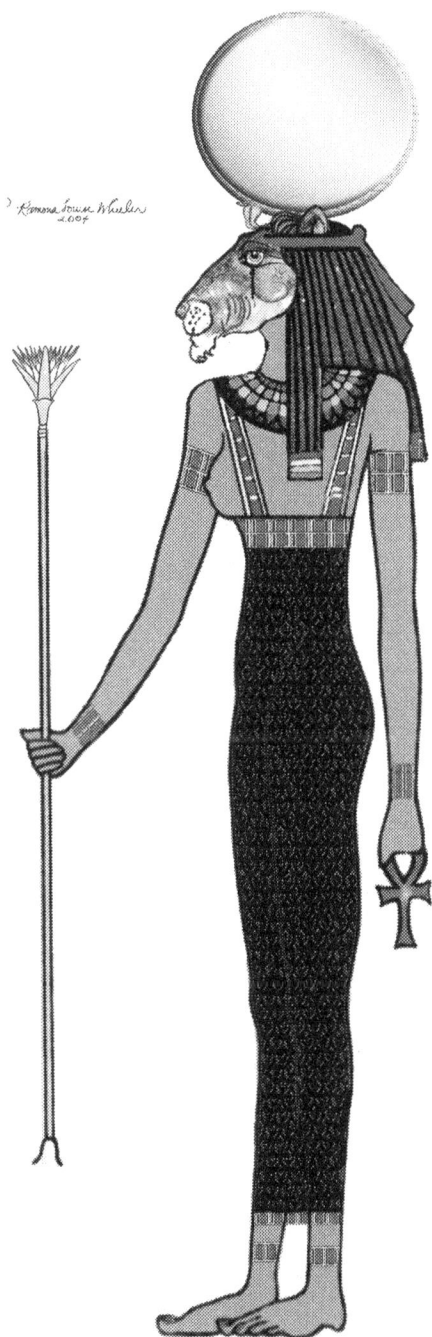

November 24   DAY ONE   ⊙ 𓏤𓏤𓏤
New Month Day   Thoth
    Be festive.

"The *naturu* and *naturitu* are festive this day. It is the feast of Ptah lifting Lord Re to heaven with his hands."

Month of Menchir begins. Festival of Little Heat (left eye of Re.)
Feast of Ptah lifting up Re with his hands.

REKEH UR

November 25   DAY TWO   ☉♀♀♀

New Crescent Day   Horus

   (Lost...)

"This is the day the *naturu* receive Re. The hearts of the Two Lands are festive."

Re returns to the sky.

REKEH UR

November 26   DAY THREE   ☉⟊⟊⟊⟊⟊

Arrival Day   Osiris

    Do not go out on any road.

"Sutekh and his confederates go out to the eastern horizon and *Ma'at* sails to where the *naturu* are."

Sutekh emerges.

November 27   DAY FOUR

Zem Priests Emerge   Isis

Honor the *naturu*. Make offerings to the spirits. Devote your whole heart to your sky *naturu*. Placate your spirits. Praise your crew on this day. (Lost...)

November 28 DAY FIVE

Altar Offerings Day Hapy

Anything you see will be good.

REKEH UR

November 29   DAY SIX

Sixth Day   Star Of His Mother

(Lost...)

"It is the day of putting up the *Djed* by Lord Osiris. The *naturu* are saddened, with their faces downcast, when they remember the majesty of him."

Feast of Isis.

November 30   DAY SEVEN   ☉♊♊♊
First Quarter Day   Qebsenuf

   Make spirit offerings. Make offerings to the *naturu*.
(Lost...)

REKEH UR

December 1

DAY EIGHT

☉⚬𝖨𝖨𝖨

Main Emergence

Ma'atef-f

  Make a holiday.

(Lost...)

Feast of the Great Heat (Right Eye Of Re). Feast of Hathor.

December 2   DAY NINE   ☉♙♙♙

Hidden One   He Does The Talking.

   Anything you see will be good.

"The *naturu* enter. He will direct this *Septy* (i.e., give rations) to all the *naturu* of *Kher-Aaha*."

Monthly feast of Re.

REKEH UR

December 3   DAY TEN   ☉𓊖𓊖𓊖

He Who Protects His Royal Name   He Makes A Name Himself.
   (Lost...)

"The *Wadjet* Eye emerges for the singing in *Innu*. It is the day they raise up the Lady Majesty in the sanctuary of Osiris. Re raises *Ma'at* again and again to Atum."

Birth of Horus the Child (son of Isis and Osiris).

REKEH UR

December 4   DAY ELEVEN   ☉♀♀♀

Great Lady Protector   Sakhmet

   You will see good from her hands.

"Feast of Neith in *Saut* (Sais.) Taking the writing material that was prepared in her house, she is guided there by Sobek."

Birth of Sobek

(*Note*: Neith serves as letter-writer for the *Naturu* in the story of Horus and Sutekh.)

REKEH UR

December 5   DAY TWELVE   ☉☽♈♈♈

Making Love   Bring The Advocate.

    Anything you see will be good.

(Lost...)

Feast of "Lifting The Sky."

REKEH UR

December 6   DAY THIRTEEN

Approach of Re   Re

   Do not go out of your house on this day.

"This day Sakhmet emerges from *Sekhemt* (Letopolis). Her great executioners pass by their offerings."

                                Monthly feast of Re.

December 7   DAY FOURTEEN   ☉☊☊☊

Progress Of The Ba   Consider The Ba.

Do not go out this day at the beginning of dawn.
"Seeing him, Sutekh kills the rebel at the bow of the great Sun Boat of Re."

December 8   DAY FIFTEEN   (Lost...)
Half Month Day   Amauai
   (Lost...)

"The *naturu* emerge with him in heaven. He holds in his hands the ankh and the scepter to the nose to *Khenty-Irety* (Horus) at the time of his reckoning."

REKEH UR

December 9   DAY SIXTEEN   (Lost...)
Two Houses Fight   Horus and Sutekh
  (Lost...)

"Awakening of Isis by the majesty of Re (lost...) their hands when Horus saved
his father. He has beaten Sutekh and his confederates."

REKEH UR

December 10   DAY SEVENTEEN   ☉♦♦♦

Second Arrival Day   Re

   (Lost...)

"It is the day of keeping those things of the *wabet* of Osiris which have been placed in the hands of Anubis."

               The day of keeping Osiris in the hands of Anubis.

REKEH UR

December 11   DAY EIGHTEEN   ☉⌂⇗⌂⇗⌂⇗

Moon Day   Ahi

   (Lost...)

"This day the seven executioners search with their fingers for the *Akhet* Eye Of Horus in the town of *Iyt* and in *Sekhemt*."

REKEH UR

December 12   DAY NINETEEN   ⊙♦⚱⟋⚱⟋

Hear His Commands   Bring His Mother.

  Do not go out by yourself in daylight.
"It is the day of mourning the *naturu*."

REKEH UR

December 13   DAY TWENTY   ☉ 𓂀𓂀𓂀

Offering Meat   Opener Of The Ways
  (Lost...)

"The Lady Majesty of Heaven goes southward."

Day of Nut.

REKEH UR

December 14   DAY TWENTY-ONE   (omission)

Apru's Day   Anubis

   (Lost...)

"It is the day of the birth of the cattle (lost...) to the place where the meadows are in the region of the foremost *naturu*."

REKEH UR

December 15   DAY TWENTY-TWO   ☉♈♈♈

Passing Of Sopdut   Nai

   Anything you see will be good.

Feasts of Horus and Ptah.

December 16   DAY TWENTY-THREE   ☉⚱⚱⚱

Last Quarter Day   Na-Ur

  Anything you see will be good.

(Lost...)

Festival of Isis.

December 17   DAY TWENTY-FOUR   ☉ ␥␥␥␥␥␥

Darkness   Nekhbet

    Do not sail on any boats. Anyone who approaches on the River will pass away. "The *naturu* are descending into the river."

Festival of Isis.

December 18   DAY TWENTY-FIVE   ⊙♄♃♂

Departing   Shem

  Anything you see will be good.

(Lost...)

REKEH UR

December 19   DAY TWENTY-SIX   (Lost...)

House Of Appearances   Ma'atef-f

(Lost...)

"It is the day of the emergence of Min from *Qebty* (Coptos.) He boasts of his beauty. Isis sees that his face is beautiful."

Feast of Min. Isis sees Osiris's face.

REKEH UR

December 20   DAY TWENTY-SEVEN   (omission)
Funerary Offerings   Khnumu

The feast of Sokar in heaven before Isis in *Ibtu*.
(omission)

Feast of Sokar. Feast of Osiris.

REKEH UR

December 21   DAY TWENTY-EIGHT   ☉⚶

Jubilee Of The Sky   Nut

(Lost...)

"Osiris is pleased. The spirits are joyful and the dead are in festivity."

The Winter Solstice.

REKEH UR

December 22   DAY TWENTY-NINE   ☉☧☧☧

Weakness   Utettef-f

Do nothing this day.

"Encouragement of fighting spawns rebellion and tumult among the children of Geb."

REKEH UR

December 23   DAY THIRTY   ☉〄〄〄〄〄

Awaken   Horus Advocates For Him.

    Do not speak loudly to anyone this day.
"Last day. House Of Re. House Of Osiris. House Of Horus."

ADDITIONAL NOTES ON THE MONTH OF MENCHIR.

REKEH UR

FAMENOTH

December 24 to January 22

Rekeh-Netches is the *naturit* of this month.

THIRD MONTH OF PORET

December 24   DAY ONE
New Month Day   Thoth

It is the day of feasting in heaven and on Earth.
"It is the feast of entering into heaven and the Two Riverbanks (Egypt). Horus is jubilant."

The month of Famenoth begins. Feast of entering heaven. Sky feast.

REKEH NETCHES

December 25   DAY TWO   ☉⚕⚕⚕

New Crescent Day   Horus

   Anything you see will be good.

(Lost...)

REKEH NETCHES

December 26   DAY THREE   (Lost...)
Arrival Day   Osiris
(Lost to papyrus damage.)

REKEH NETCHES

December 27　　　　DAY FOUR

Zem Priests Emerge　　　　　　　　　　　　　　　　　　　　　Isis
   (Lost...)

"Sutekh announces the coming conflict. His voice is so angered it is heard in heaven and on Earth."

REKEH NETCHES

December 28   DAY FIVE

Altar Offerings Day   Hapy

  Do not go out during these hours.

"Neith goes to *Saut* where they see her beauty during the night for four and one-half hours."

Festival of Lights of Neith.

REKEH NETCHES

December 29   DAY SIX   ☉♨♨♨

Sixth Day   Star Of His Mother

   Make ritual this day!

"Osiris is in the House of Osiris (Busiris). Anubis emerges with his worshippers. He receives everyone in the hall."

Procession of Anubis. Jubilation of Osiris.

REKEH NETCHES

December 30   DAY SEVEN   ☉𓊽𓆓𓊽𓆓𓊽𓆓

First Quarter Day   Qebsenuf

Do not leave your house until Re sets. Take heed of it.

"It is the day when the Eye Of Re summons his followers. They reach him at nightfall."

REKEH NETCHES

December 31   DAY EIGHT   ☉♙♙♙

Main Emergence   Ma'atef-f

    Anything you see will be good.

"It is the day of making way for the *naturu* by Khnum, who presides over those who remove themselves from him."

Festival for Khnum.

REKEH NETCHES

January 1
DAY NINE

Hidden One
(Lost...)
"Judgment in *Innu*."

He Does The Talking.

Day of Hathor.

REKEH NETCHES

January 2   DAY TEN   ☉⌂⇗⌂⇗⌂⇗

He Who Protects His Royal Name   He Makes A Name Himself.

   Any who approach her cannot be taken from her by force.

"This day Thoth comes. They guide the Great Flame into her House Of The Desert Of Eternity which has been set up for them."

Day of Thoth. Monthly feast of Re.

January 3   DAY ELEVEN   ☉⚕⚕⚕
Great Lady Protector   Sakhmet
  (Lost...)

"As to those dead who go about the *Heh* (Necropolis) this day, they do so to
repel the anger of the enemies who are in this land."

REKEH NETCHES

January 4   DAY TWELVE   ☉♀♀♀

Making Love   Bring The Advocate.

  Give food. Foodstuffs are given on this day.
"Hapy, The Nile, comes from Nun this day."

REKEH NETCHES

January 5   DAY THIRTEEN   ☉♀♀♀

Approach of Re   Re

 Any ritual performed this day will be good.

"The arrival of Thoth with his followers on this day. Replacing (lost...) in the seats of the *naturu*."

REKEH NETCHES

January 6

DAY FOURTEEN

⊙ 𓂋𓂋𓂋𓂋

Progress Of The Ba

Consider The Ba.

Do not go out on any road this day.
"It is the day of making health in *Sekhemt* (Letopolis.)"
Monthly feast of Re.

REKEH NETCHES

January 7   DAY FIFTEEN   ☉ 𓊪𓂝𓊪𓂝𓊪

Half Month Day   Amauai
   Do no work this day.
"There is uprising in the shrine."

REKEH NETCHES

January 8   DAY SIXTEEN   ☉𓂋𓏤𓂋𓏤𓂋𓏤

Two Houses Fight   Horus and Sutekh

Do not look at anything in darkness this day. Do not see darkness.
"This day they open the doors and courts of *Nest-tauy* (Karnak.)"
Day of opening the doors and courts of Karnak.

REKEH NETCHES

January 9   DAY SEVENTEEN   ⊙𒀭𒀭𒀭𒀭

Second Arrival Day   Re

  Anyone who speaks Sutekh's name will fight eternally in his house. He will not stop quarreling in his house.

(Lost...)

REKEH NETCHES

January 10
DAY EIGHTEEN

Moon Day   Ahi

   Make holiday in your house.

"It is the feast of Nut who counts the days."

Feast of Nut.

REKEH NETCHES

January 11 DAY NINETEEN (omission)
Hear His Commands Bring His Mother.
 Do not go out of your house. Do not look into the light.
"Birth of Nut anew (lost...) any dead on this day (lost...) Bastet the majesty of the foreign land."

Birth of Nut.

January 12
DAY TWENTY

Offering Meat   Opener Of The Ways

Do not go out of your house by road. Do not look into the light. (Lost...)

REKEH NETCHES

January 13   DAY TWENTY-ONE   (Lost...)
Apru's Day   Anubis
   (omission.)

REKEH NETCHES

January 14   DAY TWENTY-TWO

Passing Of Sopdut   Nai

   Do not think about or pronounce the names of snakes. It is the day of catching his children.

"Birth of the Mysterious One (Apophis) with his limbs."

Birth of Apophis.

January 15   DAY TWENTY-THREE   ☉♌♌♌

Last Quarter Day   Na-Ur
  (Lost...)
"Feast Of Horus on this day of his years in his beautiful images."
            Feast of Horus. Offerings made for the dead.

REKEH NETCHES

January 16   DAY TWENTY-FOUR

Darkness   Nekhbet

Do not go out of your house on any road. (Lost...)

REKEH NETCHES

January 17   DAY TWENTY-FIVE   (omission.)

Departing   Shem

Do nothing on this day.

"The *naturu* make a great cry in desert places on this day."

REKEH NETCHES

January 18
DAY TWENTY-SIX

⊙ 𓂀𓂋𓂋𓂋 Ma'atef-f

House Of Appearance
(Lost...)

"This day he was sent into the cave without the knowledge of the Great Ones, to look for the time of coming."

Day for those in the West.

REKEH NETCHES

January 19   DAY TWENTY-SEVEN   ☉𒀭𒀭𒀭𒀭
Funerary Offerings   Khnumu
  Do nothing on this day.
(Lost...)

REKEH NETCHES

January 20   DAY TWENTY-EIGHT   ☉♌♌♌

Jubilee Of The Sky   Nut
  (Lost...)

"The feast of Osiris in *Ibtu*. The majesty of Osiris puts up the (tree or plank) (lost...)"

Feast of Osiris.

January 21   DAY TWENTY-NINE   ☉♊♊♊
Weakness   Utettef-f
   Anything you see will be good.
(Lost...)

REKEH NETCHES

January 22 · · · · · · · · · · · · · · DAY THIRTY · · · · · · · · · · · ☉♣♣♣

Awaken · Horus Advocates For Him.
  (Lost...)
"Last day. Feast in the House Of Osiris (Busiris.) The names of the doors come into existence.
House Of Re. House Of Osiris. House Of Horus."

Festival of the Opening Of The Doorways of the Horizon. Sky feast.

REKEH NETCHES

ADDITIONAL NOTES ON THE MONTH OF FAMENOTH.

REKEH NETCHES

PARMUTHY

January 23 to February 21

Rennutet is the *naturit* of this month.

LAST MONTH OF PORET

January 23   DAY ONE   ☉↕↕↕
New Month Day   Thoth
  (Lost...)

"There is a great feast in heaven. This day they overthrow those who rebelled against their mistress."

Month of Parmuthy begins. Feast of Re.

January 24   DAY TWO   ☉⚎⚎

New Crescent Day   Horus

(Lost...)

"The majesty of Geb goes to the House Of Osiris to see Anubis who instructs the council on the day's requirements."

Procession of Geb to see Anubis.

January 25   DAY THREE   ☉𓂀𓏤𓂀𓏤𓂀
Arrival Day   Osiris

Any lion who pronounces the name of the *Sah* (Orion constellion) will die at once. Do nothing this day.

"The Great Ones fight with the Uraeus. She is appointed to create the Eye Of The Original Horus."

January 26   DAY FOUR   ⊙ 𝄞𝄞𝄞
Zem Priests Emerge   Isis

   Anything you see will be good.

"The *naturu* and *naturitu* are pleased when they see the children of Geb sitting in their places."

RENNUTET

January 27   DAY FIVE   (Lost...)

Altar Offerings Day   Hapy

Anyone who approaches on this day, anger will come of it.

"The majesty of Horus is sound when the Red One (*Wadjet*) sees his form."

RENNUTET

January 28   DAY SIX   ☉𓂋𓂧𓂋𓂧𓂋𓂧

Sixth Day   Star Of His Mother

Anyone seeing small cattle will die immediately.
"It is the going forth of the Red Star openly."
Feast of "Chewing Onions For Bastet."

January 29   DAY SEVEN   ☉☽☿

First Quarter Day   Qebsenuf

   Pay attention to the fire. Smell sweet myrrh.

"In celebration, Min goes into his tent. Life! Prosperity! Health! The *naturu* are joyous."

Feast of Min.

January 30 DAY EIGHT ☉♔♔♔

Main Emergence Ma'atef-f

(Lost...)

"The *Paut Naturu* are in adoration when they see the Eye Of The Original Horus in its place. It is perfect in all its parts, 1/2, 1/4, 1/8, 1/16, 1/32, 1/64 in the counting for its master."

Monthly feast of Re. Counting the parts of the Wadjet eye.

(*Note*: the Horus Eye was used to represent the common fractions. Horus was the *natur* of the integrity of unique identity, and each section of the Eye, or "fraction" of the whole, was a symbol for a fraction.)

RENNUTET

January 31   DAY NINE

⊙ 𓂋𓂋𓂋𓂋

Hidden One   He Does The Talking.

Do not go out in the darkness once Re sets.
(Lost...)

RENNUTET

February 1   DAY TEN   ☉♊♊♊

He Who Protects His Royal Name   He Makes A Name Himself.

Anything you see will be good.

"It is the day of introducing the Great Ones of Re to the whole *Wadjet*."

RENNUTET

February 2   DAY ELEVEN   ☉𓂭𓂭𓂭𓂭
Great Lady Protector   Sakhmet
   (Lost...)
(Lost...)

RENNUTET

February 3   DAY TWELVE   ☉𓂧𓂋𓂧𓂋𓂧𓂋

Making Love   Bring The Advocate.

Do not watch dancers or anyone who is digging the ground.

"As to him who sees dancing or digging on any roads, do not approach the majesty of *Montu*. Do not dance or dig this day."

Monthly feast of Re.

RENNUTET

February 4   DAY THIRTEEN   ☉𓂧𓂋𓂧𓂋𓂧

Approach of Re   Re

   Avoid any wind this day. Do not sail on any wind this day.
"This day they conduct Osiris on this boat to *Ibtu*."

Feast of Nut.

RENNUTET

February 5 · · · · · · · · · · · · · · DAY FOURTEEN · · · · · · · · · · ☉𓂧𓂋𓂧𓂋𓂧𓂋

Progress Of The Ba · Consider The Ba.

Do not be courageous this day.

"Re's followers go about the *naturu* in search of Sutekh's confederates."

RENNUTET

February 6
DAY FIFTEEN

⊙♁♁♁

Half Month Day   Amauai
(Lost...)

"It is a great day in the eastern horizon, where the followers of the *naturu* who are in their Houses receive their instructions before the majesty of the Great One of the Two Horizons."

RENNUTET

February 7   DAY SIXTEEN   ☉♱♱♱

Two Houses Fight   Horus and Sutekh
  Rejoice.
"This day Khopry hears the words of his followers. Every town rejoices."
Procession of Khepry.

RENNUTET

February 8   DAY SEVENTEEN   ☉𓂋𓂋𓂋

Second Arrival Day   Re

  (Lost...)

"Sutekh, son of Nut, emerges to disturb the Great Ones who restrain him in his town. Now these *naturu* who recognized him drive away his followers. None of them remain."

Procession of Sutekh.

February 9   DAY EIGHTEEN

Moon Day   Ahi

Do not approach in the morning. Do not wash yourself with water. "Do not approach when the majesty of Re emerges."

RENNUTET

February 10   DAY NINETEEN   ☉♈♈♈

Hear His Commands   Bring His Mother.

  Anything you see will be good.

"The majesty of Re emerges in his Sun Boat to feast in *Innu*."

Feast of Re.

RENNUTET

February 11 DAY TWENTY ☉ 𓂀𓃀𓂀𓃀𓂀

Offering Meat Opener Of The Ways

The soul of anyone who passes rebels will suffer from weakness for eternity.
Do not work.

"He casts down those who rebel against their master."

RENNUTET

February 12   DAY TWENTY-ONE

Apru's Day   Anubis

Do not go out of your house on any road this day.
(Lost...)

February 13   DAY TWENTY-TWO   ⊙ 〔hieroglyphs〕

Passing Of Sopdut   Nai

Anyone born this day will not live.

"It is the day of slaying the children of rebellion."

RENNUTET

February 14   DAY TWENTY-THREE

Last Quarter Day   Na-Ur

  (Lost...)

"It is the day of offering foodstuff in *Ibtu* to the spirits."

February 15   DAY TWENTY-FOUR   ☉⌂⌂⌂⌂⌂

Darkness   Nekhbet

Do not say Sutekh's name. Should you forget and do so, you will have quarreling in your home forever.

"It is the day Sutekh rises up against Osiris."

RENNUTET

February 16   DAY TWENTY-FIVE   ☉𝄞𝄞𝄞𝄞𝄞

Departing   Shem

Do not eat anything which is on or which swims in the water.
"It is the day they cut the tongue from Sobek."

(Note: the tongue is is for the murder of the ferryman *Inty.)*

RENNUTET

February 17   DAY TWENTY-SIX   (Lost...)

House Of Appearance   Ma'atef-f

    (Lost to papyrus damage.)

RENNUTET

February 18   DAY TWENTY-SEVEN   ☉ 🐍🐍🐍

Funerary Offerings   Khnumu

Do not go out until Re sets.

"Sakhmet is angry in the land of *Temhu* (or *tenu*) Behold! She went about walking."

Feast of Sakhmet destroying mankind.

RENNUTET

February 19   DAY TWENTY-EIGHT   ☉♚♚♚

Jubilee Of The Sky   Nut

   Anything you see will be good.

(Lost...)

RENNUTET

February 20   DAY TWENTY-NINE   ☉♨♨♨

Weakness   Utettef-f

It will be pleasant on this day. Offer myrrh to your sky *naturu*.
"The *naturu* are pleased when they give praise to Osiris. There is incense on the fire."

Adoration of Beautiful Being (Osiris.) Sky Feast.

RENNUTET

February 21   DAY THIRTY   ☉♜♜♜

Awaken   Horus Advocates For Him.

   Make offerings to all the *naturu*.

"Last day. Make offerings to Ptah-Sokar-Osir. (Lost...) Re, Lord of the Dual
Dimensions of *Innu* this day. Offer to all *naturu* this day.
House Of Re. House Of Osiris. House Of Horus."

   Offerings to Re, Osiris, Horus, Ptah, and Sokar.

RENNUTET

Additonal Notes on the Month of Parmuthy:

RENNUTET

Khonsu is the *natur* of this month.

FIRST MONTH OF SHOMU

February 22   DAY ONE   ⊙☥☥☥

New Month Day   Thoth

   Anything you see this day will be good.

"Feast of Horus, Son of Isis, and his followers this day."

               First Day of Pachons. Feast for Re, Horus and Renemutet.

February 23   DAY TWO   ☉ 𓂋𓂋𓂋𓂋𓂋

New Crescent Day   Horus

    Do not sail on this day in any wind.

(Lost...)

February 24   DAY THREE   ☉♌♌♌
Arrival Day   Osiris
   Anything you see this day will be good.
(Lost...)

KHONSU

February 25   DAY FOUR   ☉𓂀𓂀𓂀

Zem Priests Emerge   Isis

     Do not go out of your house.

"It is the day of (Lost...) follow Horus this day."

February 26   DAY FIVE   ⊙𓂋𓏤𓂋𓏤𓂋𓏤

Altar Offerings Day   Hapy

Anyone who goes out of his house will waste away from disease until he dies. "This day is the Feast Of The Golden *Ba* (*Ba* Of Osiris)."

Feast of Sexual fertility of Min.

February 27   DAY SIX   ☉♊♊♊

Sixth Day   Star Of His Mother

   Anything you see this day will be good.

"The Great Ones and their followers arrive from the House Of Re, rejoicing as they receive the *Wadjet* Eye."

        Harvest festival. Festival of the Great One of the House Of Re.

February 28   DAY SEVEN   ☉♉♉♉

First Quarter Day   Qebsennuf

   Every heart is glad. The land is happy.

"The crew follows Horus into the foreign land. There he examines the List and smites those who rebelled against their master."

March 1   DAY EIGHT   (Lost...)
Main Emergence   Ma'atet-f
   Anything you see this day will be good.
(Lost...)

Festival of Isis.

KHONSU

March 2   DAY NINE   ☉♨♨♨

Hidden One   He Does The Talking.

   Anything you see this day will be good.

(Lost...)

Monthly feast of Re.

March 3   DAY TEN   ⊙🔲🔲🔲🔲🔲

He Protects His Royal Name   He Makes His Name Himself.

"The White One Of Heaven goes upstream to search among those who rebelled gainst their master in the Delta."

(Lost...)

Festival Of Clothing Anubis.

March 4   DAY ELEVEN   (Lost...)
Great Lady Protector   Sakhmet
(Lost...)
(Lost...)

KHONSU

March 5   DAY TWELVE   ☉ 𓂋𓆓𓂋𓆓𓂋𓆓
Making Love   Bring The Advocate.
(Day lost...)

KHONSU

March 6   DAY THIRTEEN   (Lost...)

Approach Of Re   Re

(Day lost to papyrus damage...)

Monthly feast of Re.

KHONSU

March 7   DAY FOURTEEN   ☉ 𓂀𓂀𓂀𓂀

Progress Of The Ba   Consider The Ba.

"(Lost...) Apophis in (lost...) They cut the tongue of the enemy of Sobek."
The day of cutting out the tongue of Sobek, the crocodile natur.

March 8   DAY FIFTEEN   (Lost...)

Half Month Day   Armauai

(Day lost to papyrus damage...)

KHONSU

March 9   DAY SIXTEEN

Two Houses Fight   Horus and Sutekh

Anyone born this day will die. Do not go out of your house until Re sets in the horizon.

(Lost...)

March 10   DAY SEVENTEEN   ☉♙♙♙

Second Arrival Day   Re

   Anything you see this day will be good..

(Lost...)

KHONSU

March 11   DAY EIGHTEEN   ☉⚍⚌

Moon Day   Ahi

Anything you see this day will be good.

"The *Paut Naturu* is joyous and the crew of Re makes merry."

Day of joy for Re and his Paut Naturu.

KHONSU

March 12   DAY NINETEEN   ☉⚇

Hear His Commands   Bring His Mother.
   (Lost...)

"This day Thoth counts in the presence of Re, who hears the Great One Of Reality."

The day of the counting of Thoth.

March 13   DAY TWENTY   ☉ 𓂀𓂀𓂀
Offering Meat   Opener Of The Ways
   (Lost...)
"Ma'at judges in the presence of the *naturu* in the island sanctuary of Sakhmet
(Letopolis,) who become angered.
The Lord Horus changes it."

Ma'at judges souls.

March 14   DAY TWENTY-ONE   ☉⌂⌐⌂⌐⌂⌐

Apru's Day   Anubis

  (Lost...)

"Vomit up the things that returned with the boat, so that no follower of Re remains who was in attendance."

KHONSUI

March 15   DAY TWENTY-TWO   ☉♙♙♙

Passing Of Sopdut   Nai

Anyone born on this day will live to old age.

(Lost...)

March 16   DAY TWENTY-THREE   ☉♦♦♦

Last Quarter Day   Na-Ur

   Anything you see this day will be good.

(Lost...)

KHONSU

March 17   DAY TWENTY-FOUR   (Lost...)

Darkness   Nekhbet

(Day lost to papyrus damage...)

March 18   DAY TWENTY-FIVE   (Lost...)
Departing   Shem
(Day lost to papyrus damage...)

KHONSU

March 19   DAY TWENTY-SIX   ☉♈♈♈

House Of Appearances   Ma'atef-f

  Anything you see this day will be good.

(Lost...)

KHONSU

March 20   DAY TWENTY-SEVEN
Funerary Offerings   Khnum
(Lost...)

March 21   DAY TWENTY-EIGHT   ☉♀♀♀

Jubilee Of The Sky   Nut

Anything you see this day will be good. (Lost...)

The Spring Equinox.

March 22   DAY TWENTY-NINE   (Lost...)

Weakness   Utettef-f

(Day lost to papyrus damage...)

KHONSU

March 23   DAY THIRTY   ☉♌♌♌

Awaken   Horus Advocates For Him.
(Lost...)
"Last Day (lost...)
House Of Re, House Of Osiris, House Of Horus."
Celebrations for Re, Osiris, and Horus.

Additonal Notes on the Month of Pachons:

KHONSU

PAONY

Khenthy is the *natur* of this month.

SECOND MONTH OF SHOMU

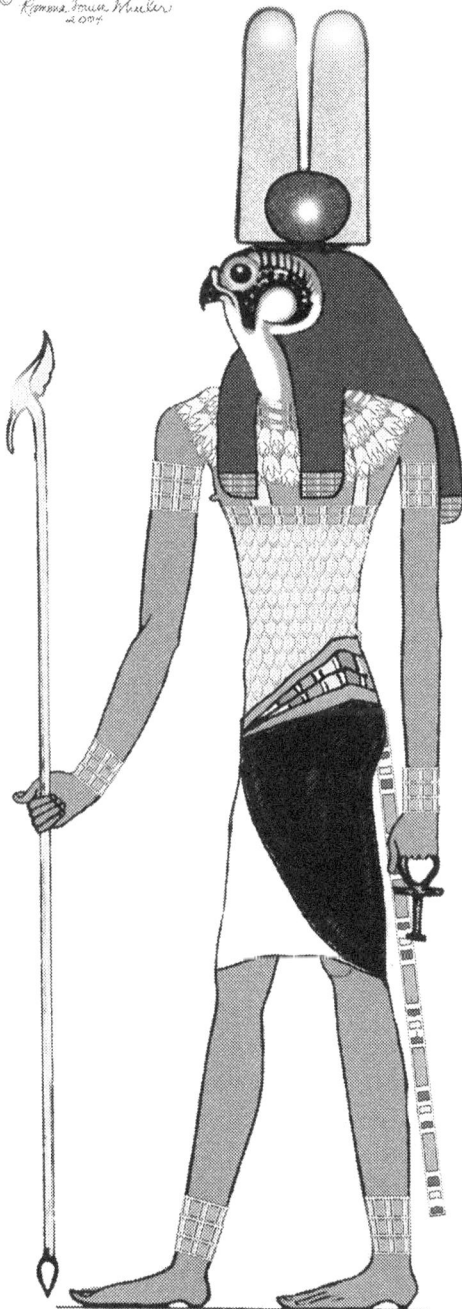

March 24

DAY ONE

⊙☥☥☥

New Month Day

Thoth

(Lost...)

The Month of Paony begins. Feasts for Re, Horus and Bastet.

KHENTHY

March 25   DAY TWO   (omission)
New Crescent Day   Horus
   (omission...)
"The hearts of the *naturu* listen very well. The crew of Re is in celebration."
                        Holy to Re and his followers.

KHENTHY

March 26
Arrival Day
(Lost...)

DAY THREE

☉♁♉♉

Osiris

"The followers of Re fix this day in heaven as a feast."

KHENTHY

March 27   DAY FOUR

Zem Priests Emerge   Isis

   Anything you see this day will be good.

(Lost...)

KHENTHY

March 28   DAY FIVE   ☉♁♁♁

Altar Offerings Day   Hapy

Shout at no one on this day.

"That which Geb and Nut have done is counted in the presence of the *naturu*."

KHENTHY

March 29   DAY SIX   (omission...)
Sixth Day   Star Of His Mother
   (Lost...)

"Horus goes to avenge what was done against his father and to question the followers of his father Osiris on this day."

KHENTHY

March 30   DAY SEVEN   ☉𝄃𝄃𝄃𝄃

First Quarter Day   Qebsennuf

While Re is in the horizon (during waking time) do not go out of your house. "It is the day that the executioners of Sakhmet (*khatbu*) count by names."

Feast Of The Wadjet Eye.

KHENTHY

March 31   DAY EIGHT   ☉♈♈♈

Main Emergence   Ma'atet-f

Make a holiday for Re and his followers on this day. Make this a good day. (Lost...)

KHENTHY

April 1   DAY NINE   ☉♟♟♟
Hidden One   He Does The Talking.

Make different kinds of incense from sweet herbs for the followers of Re. This will please him today.

(Lost...)

Feast of Re.

KHENTHY

April 2   DAY TEN   ☉ 𓈖𓂝𓈖𓂝𓈖𓂝

He Protects His Royal Name   He Makes His Name Himself.

   Those born on this day will be noble.

(Lost...)

KHENTHY

April 3
DAY ELEVEN

☉⌂⌂⌂⌂⌂

Great Lady Protector

Sakhmet

Do not sail this day. Anyone who sails on the river won't live. "It is the day of catching birds and fish by the followers of Re."

KHENTHY

April 4   DAY TWELVE   Bring The Advocate.

Making Love

   Anything you see this day will be good.

KHENTHY

April 5   DAY THIRTEEN   ☉♌♌♌
Approach Of Re   Re
  Make offerings.
"Feast of the *Wadjet* Eye. Her followers are also in festival when singing and chanting on the day of offering incense and all manner of sweet herbs."

Feast Of Re.

April 6   DAY FOURTEEN   ☉♨♨♨

Progress Of The Ba   Consider The Ba.

  Anything you see this day will be good.

(Lost...)

KHENTHY

April 7   DAY FIFTEEN

Half Month Day   Armauai

    Do not judge yourself. It is the day of fighting (lost...) their rebellion. (Lost to papyrus damage...)

KHENTHY

April 8   DAY SIXTEEN   ☉♨♨♨

Two Houses Fight   Horus and Sutekh

Anyone born this day will die as a great magistrate to all people.
(Lost...)

KHENTHY

April 9
DAY SEVENTEEN

Second Arrival Day
Re

Do not go out. Do not do anything on this day. Do no work.
(Lost...)

KHENTHY

April 10   DAY EIGHTEEN   ☉𓂃𓂃𓂃
Moon Day   Ahi

Do not eat the meat of lions. Any who smell the stench of death, and has a skin, will never be healthy.

"It is the day of the emergence of *Khenty (Osiris)* from the *naturu's* house, when he goes on to the august mountain."

Feast of Osiris.

April 11   DAY NINETEEN

Hear His Commands   Bring His Mother.

If you see a lion, he will pass away.

"The *Paut Naturu* sails throughout the land. There are many departures of the *Paut Naturu* throughout the land on this day. This day is day of the judging of the Great Ones."

KHENTHY

April 12   DAY TWENTY   ⊙𓂋𓂧𓂋𓂧𓂋𓂧

Offering Meat   Opener Of The Ways

Do not sail in any wind this day.

"Many die because they come on an unfavorable wind."

KHENTHY

April 13   DAY TWENTY-ONE   ☉◖◻◿◻◿◈

Apru's Day   Anubis

Stay in until Re appears on his horizon.

"It is the day of the living-legs, the children of Nut."

Feast of the Children of Nut.

(*Note*: The Yearly Five Days are the children of Nut, her limbs, as in a family tree.)

KHENTHY

April 14   DAY TWENTY-TWO

Passing Of Sopdut   Nai

Do not go out on this day.

"There is a disturbance below, and turmoil among the *naturu* of the *ka*-shrines on this day, when Shu finds fault with the Great Ones of infinity."

KHENTHY

April 15

DAY TWENTY-THREE

⊙♙♙♙

Last Quarter Day

Na-Ur

(Lost...)

"The crew rest when they see the enemy of their master."

KHENTHY

April 16   DAY TWENTY-FOUR   ☉👥

Darkness   Nekhbet

　Anything you see this day will be good.

(Lost to papyrus damage...)

KHENTHY

April 17   DAY TWENTY-FIVE   ☉⚱⚱⚱
Departing   Shem
  (Lost...)

"The *Akhet* Eye pacifies everything and everyone. It is pleasant to the *naturu*."
                              Holy to Re.

KHENTHY

April 18   DAY TWENTY-SIX   ☉ ꞉꞉꞉꞉꞉꞉

House Of Appearances   Ma'atef-f
    (Lost...)

"Neith goes forth walking in the flood this day, searching for the things of Sobek. If a lion sees them, he will pass away."

Procession of Neith.

KHENTHY

April 19　　　　　DAY TWENTY-SEVEN　⊙𓂋𓂋𓂋

Funerary Offerings　　　　　　　　　　　　　　Khnum

　Do not work on this day.

"There is fighting among the *naturu* this day, with the cutting of heads and the binding of the necks. "

KHENTHY

April 20   DAY TWENTY-EIGHT   ☉♣♣♣

Jubilee Of The Sky   Nut

Act in acordance with the events of the day.

"It is the day of purifying things and making offerings in the House Of Osiris."

Day of purifying all things.

KHENTHY

April 21   DAY TWENTY-NINE   (Lost...)
Weakness   Utettef-f
  Anything you see this day will be good.
(Lost to papyrus damage...)

KHENTHY

April 22   DAY THIRTY   ☉♀♀♀

Awaken   Horus Advocates For Him.

(Lost...)

"Last Day. The emergence of Osiris in the form of Shu, with the intention of bringing back the *Wadjet* Eye. This day Thoth appeases her.
House Of Re. House Of Osiris. House of Horus."

Holy to Thoth. Feast of Re.

KHENTHY

ADDITIONAL NOTES ON THE MONTH OF PAONY:

KHENTHY

EPIPY

Ipt is the *natur* of this month.

THIRD MONTH OF SHOMU

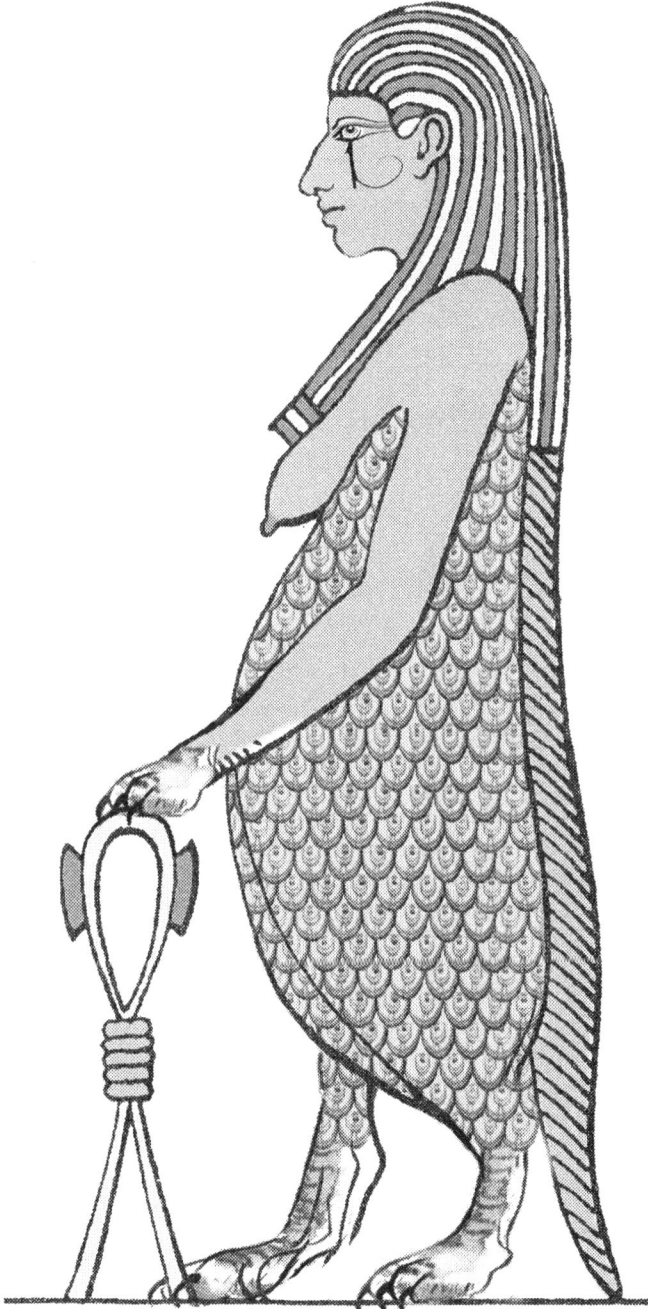

April 23   DAY ONE   ☉⚷⚷⚷

New Month Day   Thoth

(Lost...)

"There is a great feast in the southern heaven for Hathor, Mistress Of Heaven, and everyone and everything are festive."

Month of Epipy begins. Festivals to Hathor and Bastet.

Day of the great feast of the southern heavens for Re.

April 24   DAY TWO   ☉♌

New Crescent Day   Horus
(Lost...)

"The *naturu* and *naturitu* spend the day in festivity, and in great astonishment in the sacred House Of The *Naturu*."

The naturitu feast in their Houses Of Life.

April 25   DAY THREE   ⊙𓂋𓂋𓂋

Arrival Day   Osiris

   Do nothing on this day.

"The divine majesty is angered."

(Note: this refers to Hathor, in her form as the *Wadjet* Eye.)

April 26   DAY FOUR   Isis

Zem Priests Emerge

  Anything you see this day will be good.

(Lost...)

April 27
DAY FIVE

Altar Offerings Day   Hapy

Do not go out. Do not sail or proceed by boat. Do no work.

"It is the day of the departure of this *naturit* (Hathor) to the place from where she came. The *naturu* are downcast."

Hathor sails for Punt.

(*Note*: Feast of the Beautiful Reunion. Hathor's Boat leaves Dendera and sails to Horus in Edfu. She visits the House Of the *naturit* Mut. She ends her travels at the great House Of Horus. The two statues are enshrined together for 14 days, then taken to the roof of the House Of The *Natur* to greet Re.)

April 28   DAY SIX

Sixth Day   Star Of His Mother

Do not fight or make uproar in your house.
"Every House Of The *Naturit* (Hathor) is in like manner."

April 29   DAY SEVEN   ☉ 𓃀𓏤𓃀𓏤𓃀𓏤

First Quarter Day   Qebsennuf
  (Lost...)

"The *naturu* sail after the *naturit* (Hathor.) There is great flame in front of them."
The other naturu follow.

April 30   DAY EIGHT

Main Emergence   Ma'atet-f

Do not strike anyone. Do not beat anyone this day.
"This day the followers of the majesty of the *naturit* are slaughtered."

May 1   DAY NINE   ☉♁♁♁
Hidden One   He Does The Talking.
   (Lost...)

"The *naturu* are content and all are happy. Re is at peace with the *Akhet* Eye Of Horus. All the *naturu* are in celebration this day."

May 2   DAY TEN   ☉𓂀𓂀𓂀

He Protects His Royal Name   He Makes His Name Himself.
  (Lost...)

"Creating enmity (hostility) over the event. The *naturu* who are in the shrine are sad."

Monthly feast of Re.

May 3   DAY ELEVEN   ☉𓂝𓏲𓂝𓏲𓂝𓏲

Great Lady Protector   Sakhmet

   Do not perform any rituals this day.

"Bring the Great Ones to the booth. Re makes known to them what he observed through the Eye of Horus The Elder. They bow their heads when they see the Eye of Horus being angry before Re."

May 4   DAY TWELVE   ☉♊♊♊

Making Love   Bring The Advocate.
  "Holiday (lost...) reception of Re. His followers are all festive."
(Lost...)

May 5   DAY THIRTEEN   ☉⌂⌂⌂⌂⌂

Approach Of Re   Re
  (Lost...)
"The majesty of the *naturu* sails west to see the beauty of Osiris."

IPT

May 6   DAY FOURTEEN

Progress Of The Ba   Consider The Ba.

 Do not burn in your house anything of burning flame, with its glow.
"On this day of the anger of the Eye Of The Original Horus."

May 7   DAY FIFTEEN   ☉♌

Half Month Day   Armauai

   Anything you see this day will be good. You will see every good thing in your house.

"This day Horus hears your words in the presence of all the *naturu* and *naturitu*."

Horus hears the supplications of the naturu.

IPT

May 8   DAY SIXTEEN

Two Houses Fight   Horus and Sutekh

  (Lost...)

"It is the day the majesty of Re in *Innu* sends *Ma'at* out to the shrine. The *naturu* learn why he is angry. She is blamed."

Ma'at appears before Re.

May 9   DAY SEVENTEEN   ☉𐍂𐍂𐍂𐍂𐍂

Second Arrival Day   Re
  (Lost...)

"The escape of the fugitive (Eye) and the *naturu* are deprived of Re, who had come to hand the rebels over to them."

May 10   DAY EIGHTEEN   ☉⎆⎆⎆⎆
Moon Day   Ahi

   Do not travel by road. Do not go out of your house. Anyone who is outside (lost...) the trampling of a bull.
"*Ma'at* and Re go forth in secret."

Ma'at and Re leave in secret.

May 11   DAY NINETEEN   ☉ 𓂀𓂀𓂀𓂀

Hear His Commands   Bring His Mother.

Do not embrace anyone a second time nor do any work.

(Lost...)

May 12   DAY TWENTY
Offering Meat   Opener Of The Ways

  Do not go out on any road this day.
(Lost...).

May 13   DAY TWENTY-ONE   ☉⚱⚱⚱

Apru's Day   Anubis

  Anything you see this day will be good.

May 14   DAY TWENTY-TWO

Passing Of Sopdut   Nai

Do not look at anyone with fevers or rashes. Do not watch anyone digging this day.

"It is the day of the coming of Sepa of In to *Innu*."

(*Note*: *Sepa* is a reptile-*natur*, chief of the seven spirits who guard Osiris.)

May 15   DAY TWENTY-THREE   ☉ 🔆🔆🔆🔆

Last Quarter Day   Na-Ur

   Anyone born on this day will die.

"It is the day of quarrelling and being reproached by Osiris."

May 16   DAY TWENTY-FOUR   ☉⣿

Darkness   Nekhbet
    (Lost...)

"It is the day of (lost...) children of rebellion. The *naturu* have slain them because he came and then he sailed south."

May 17   DAY TWENTY-FIVE

Departing   Shem

  Do not go out at midday.

"The great enemy (Apophis) is in the House Of Life Of Sakhmet."

May 18   DAY TWENTY-SIX   ☉♈♈♈

House Of Appearances   Ma'atef-f

    Anything you see this day will be good.

(Lost...)

May 19   DAY TWENTY-SEVEN

Funerary Offerings   Khnum

(Lost...)

"It is the day of sailing on the river, and of overthrowing the enclosure wall."

May 20   DAY TWENTY-EIGHT   ☉𓂋𓂋𓂋

Jubilee Of The Sky   Nut
(Lost...)

"Creating misery and bringing fear into agreement with the habit of this time of year."

(Note: this passage refers to the Nile's lowest water levels of the year)

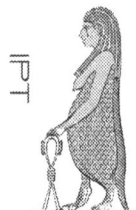

May 21   DAY TWENTY-NINE   ☉𝌆
Weakness   Utettef-f

It is the day of feeding the *naturit* and her followers.
"This day is the feast of Mut in *Sheta*."

Festival of Mut. Sky feast.

IPT

May 22   DAY THIRTY   ☉↯↯↯

Awaken   Horus Advocates For Him.

   Anything you see this day will be good.

"Last Day. House Of Re. House Of Osiris. House Of Horus."

Ceremony of Horus Of The Winged Disk.

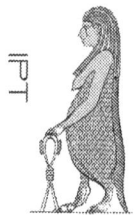

Additional Notes on the Month of Epipy.

Horus Of The Two Horizons is the *natur* of this Month.

FINAL MONTH OF SHOMU

May 23   DAY ONE   ☉𓎹

New Month Day   Thoth

   This day is the feast of Osiris.

"Send *Aabt*-offerings to those who are in heaven. All the *naturu* and *naturitu* spend the day in feasting Osiris."

Month of Mesore begins. Festivals for Re.

HORUS

May 24   DAY TWO   ☉ 👁👁👁

New Crescent Day   Horus
   (Lost...)

"Ma'at (lost...) and all the *naturu* perform the rites as one who is in heaven."
Sacred to Ma'at.

May 25   DAY THREE   ⊙ 🏛🏛🏛🏛🏛

Arrival Day   Osiris

Do not go out and do nothing on this day.

"The majesty of this *naturit* proceeds to *Innu*. A feast was made on this day."

Feast of Raet. Feast of Hathor as Sopdut.

May 26   DAY FOUR   ⊙◌◌◌◌

Zem Priests Emerge   Isis
   (Lost...)

"It is the day of the procession of *Sopdut* and her followers, being in a state of youth and remaining in the course of the day. She will never be able to find a living soul... (lost...)'

Processional Day of Sopdut.

May 27   DAY FIVE   ☉♈♈♈♈

Altar Offerings Day   Hapy

  Anything you see this day will be good.

"*Maner* (the name of Min's sanctuary) is in festivity, Min being at *Khent-min*."

Day of the appearance of Min.

(*Note*: *Khent-min* was known as Panopolis, and is now called *Akhmim*.)

HORUS

May 28   DAY SIX   ☉ 🏺🏺🏺

Sixth Day   Star Of His Mother

Do nothing on this day.
"Send the restored one into Mouth Of The Far Horizon, and hide the mysteries of the conspirators on this day."

May 29   DAY SEVEN   ☉𓎡𓃀𓎡𓃀𓎡
First Quarter Day   Qebsennuf

   Any who draws near him will be trampled by a bull and die.
"The Dead One goes about the Heh and appears on Earth."
                    Anubis travels to the necropolis.

May 30   DAY EIGHT   ☉⚇

Main Emergence   Ma'atet-f

  Anything you see this day will be good.

(Lost...)

Wadjet's Summer Solstice.

HORUS

May 31   DAY NINE   ☉♌♌♌
Hidden One   He Does The Talking.

Those born today will possess noble honor.
(Lost...)

June 1   DAY TEN   ☉⦶

He Protects His Royal Name   He Makes His Name Himself.
     (Lost...)

"This day the crew in the Delta is repulsed. It is the day the Eye Of Re enters the horizon when he sees his beauty."

Monthly feast of Re. Holiday of Anubis.

HORUS

June 2   DAY ELEVEN   ☉𓂋𓏥𓂋𓏥

Great Lady Protector   Sakhmet

   Do not perform any rituals this day.
"There is disturbance in the presence of Re's followers and the driving back of
the confederates of Sutekh into the eastern country."

June 3   DAY TWELVE   ☉⚬⚱⚱⚱

Making Love   Bring The Advocate.

   (Lost...)

"There is joy throughout the whole world on this day. The hearts of those in the shrine are happy."

HORUS

June 4   DAY THIRTEEN   ☉♊♊♊

Approach Of Re   Re
  (Lost...)

"It is a holiday because of defending the son of Osiris. (Lost...) at the portal by Sutekh."

Feast of the followers of Horus.

June 5   DAY FOURTEEN   ☉𝍷𝍷𝍷

Progress Of The Ba   Consider The Ba.
  (Lost...)

"Establish her throne and hall (lost...) the *naturu's* portal for the first time on this day."

HORUS

June 6   DAY FIFTEEN   ⊙◻➘◻➘◻➘

Half Month Day   Armauai

  (Lost...)

"Re emerges on this day to appease Nun (lost...) in his cavern, in the presence of his followers and the *Paut Naturu* of the Evening Boat Of The Sun."

Re emerges to honor Nun.

June 7   DAY SIXTEEN   ☉♍

Two Houses Fight   Horus and Sutekh

   Ritually give water to those ancestors who are in the West.

"(Lost...) *Paut Naturu* of the West. It is pleasant to your divine Father and Mother who are in the *Heh.*"

June 8   DAY SEVENTEEN   ⊙♀♀♀
Second Arrival Day   Re
  Anything you see this day will be good. (Lost...)

HORUS

June 9   DAY EIGHTEEN   ⊙𓂭𓂭𓂭𓂭

Moon Day   Ahi

Do not go out during the morning. Any lions that go out will be blind and will not live.

"The crew who is leading the rebels. If any lion goes out on top of the Earth this day, he will go blind and they say he will not live."

HORUS

June 10   DAY NINETEEN   ☉♨

Hear His Commands   Bring His Mother.

  Feast your nome *Naturu.* Placate your spirits.

"Appease your spirit, for the *Wadjet* Eye of Horus has returned complete. Nothing is missing from it."

Day of the return of the complete Eye Of Re (Wadjet eye).

HORUS

June 11   DAY TWENTY
Offering Meat   Opener Of The Ways

   Kill no *inhy*-reptiles this day.
"It is the day of the purification and transformation of the noble ones. There is silence on Earth because of it, to appease the *Wadjet* Eye."

(*Note*: *inhy*-reptiles protect the dead. Killing one would be killing a divine creature.)

June 12   DAY TWENTY-ONE   ☉♔♔♔

Apru's Day   Anubis

  Anything you see this day will be good.

(Lost...)

June 13   DAY TWENTY-TWO   ☉♈♈♈

Passing Of Sopdut   Nai

   (Lost...)

"The feast of Anubis, who is on his mountain this day. The children of Geb
and Nut spend the day in festivity, which is a holiday after the good bath of the
naturu."

Anubis feasts with the children of Nut and Geb.

June 14

DAY TWENTY-THREE

Last Quarter Day   Na Ur

Eat no bread and drink no beer this day. Do not taste bread or beer. "Because of what was done before him who rebelled against his master on this day."

HORUS

June 15   DAY TWENTY-FOUR   ☉♈♈♈

Darkness   Nekhbet

   Make offerings to Re. Make a holiday in your house this day.
"Make *aabet*-offerings to the *naturu* in the presence of Re."

June 16   DAY TWENTY-FIVE   ☉⚱⚱⚱
Departing   Shem
  (Lost...)

"The *naturu* are established in front of the crew of Re, who is happy in the *Hiwet*-desert."

June 17   DAY TWENTY-SIX

House Of Appearances   Ma'atef-f

   Stay in at midday. Do not go out of your house at midday. "The *naturu* sail with all winds. (Lost...)"

June 18   DAY TWENTY-SEVEN   ⊙𓂝𓂝𓂝

Funerary Offerings   Khnum

  Do not do anything this day.

(Lost...)

HORUS

June 19   DAY TWENTY-EIGHT   ☉♁♁♁

Jubilee Of The Sky   Nut

  Anything you see this day will be good.

"(Lost...) feast of Min."

Feast day of Min.

HORUS

June 20   DAY TWENTY-NINE   ☉ꭰꭰꭰ

Weakness   Utettef-f

   (Lost...)

'There is a holiday in the House Of Sokar, in the estate of Ptah. Those who are in his estate are in great festivity, being healthy ... (lost...)"

Feast in the House Of Life Of Sokar. Feast of Ptah.

June 21 DAY THIRTY ☉♈♈♈

Awaken Horus Advocates For Him.

Rites performed or anyone born on this day, or anything done this day, will be good all year. Make numerous offerings, and sing this day.

"Last Day. Anything that comes from the estate of Ptah will be good. House Of Re. House Of Osiris. House Of Horus."

Birthday Of Re. Final Day Of The Year.. Summer Solstice.

HORUS

ADDITONAL NOTES:

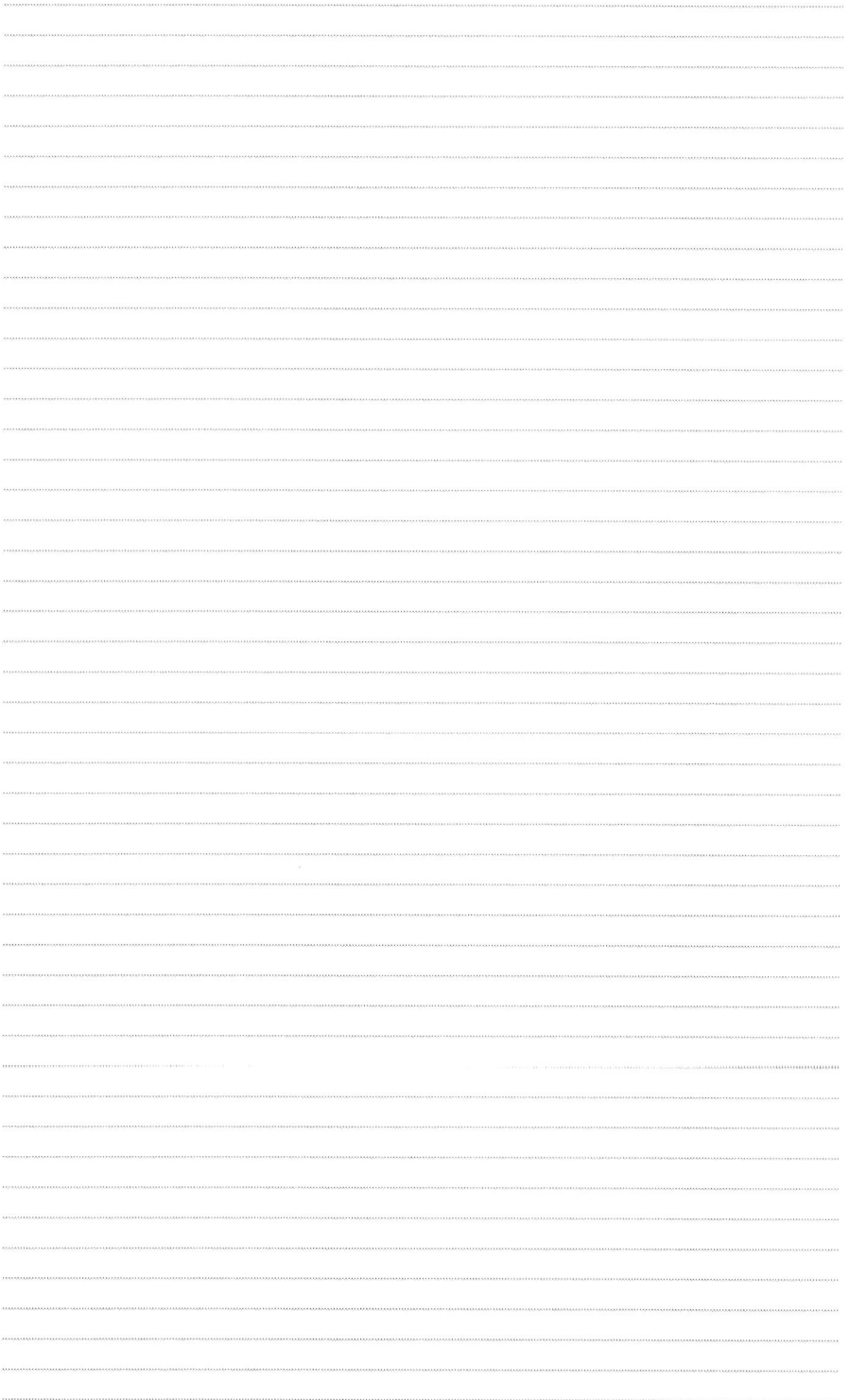

Leap Year Day:

www.ingramcontent.com/pod-product-compliance
Lightning Source LLC
Chambersburg PA
CBHW031230090426
42742CB00007B/146